D1580121

A WANDERER IN NORTH WALES

CLEDWYN HUGHES

A WANDERER
IN NORTH WALES

CLEDWYN HUGHES

*Drawings & Engravings
by John Petts*

PHOENIX HOUSE LONDON

NOVELS BY THE SAME AUTHOR

The Different Drummer

The Inn Closes for Christmas

Wennon

The Civil Strangers
[In preparation]

Made 1949 in Great Britain
Printed at Rochester by The Stanhope Press Limited for
PHOENIX HOUSE LIMITED
38 William IV Street, London

First published in Great Britain 1949

THE FOUR PARTS

Bibliography and Index
(*see page 191*)

ILLUSTRATIONS

Part I

Part II

Part III

Part IV

For permission to reproduce the drawing on page 72 and the wood-
engravings on pp. 56, 114, 123, 146, 149 our acknowledgments and
thanks are due to The Caseg Press, Llanystumdwy, North Wales

I. THE BORDER AND THE PARADISE

THE BORDER AND THE PARADISE

Come to North Wales, say the posters. An abbey gently ruined, Bala Lake in the sunshine. Or the choir at the Eisteddfod, so sweet, theatrical in the costume. Take salmon from the Dee, the sunrise from Snowdon. Be another Lady of Llangollen. Trains are fast to Colwyn Bay and the line goes straight to Holyhead. And from there lies Dublin, another world west with the steamer. Come to North Wales and climb Cader Idris. But stay not there the night. For if you do you will surely wake a madman or a corpse or a poet. Come to lush mid-Wales. Or to Bardsey, lonely island where the seals breed and the saints lie ever sleeping. Walk the pilgrim way down the Lleyn Peninsula. Or round Anglesey, last island home of the Druids, mistletoe, and the curving blade.

Only one way into North Wales. One way only to reach the valley of Conway and the Clwyd, the moors of Denbighshire. The strange, uneasy Menai Straits, and the bird island of Puffin, blue by Dutchman's Bank.

Over the Border. Slip easy into Wales. There is no painted post or swinging chain. No sudden sweet Welsh voice. No sudden end of listening, no entry to a land of sudden singing. Into North Wales from farming Cheshire or rolling, wooded Shropshire. Into Montgomeryshire, scattered, and with the gentle hills. Or into Denbighshire, the earth black, and the white-eyed miners singing in the buses.

Once here the Welsh Marches. Norman castles at Chester, Shrewsbury, Ludlow, with the Lords Marchers living in power.

And Offa and his Dyke. Levelled now in the many places. But still rising green and used by the cows to promenade, by boys in summer.

Roman days. Roads straight from the level Border. Up to the tops of the hills. Lanes now, and neglected, walked only by the sheep and the postmen. Life lies now in the valley and the road must wind and twist and turn. Have the little hawthorn and the hazel corners, and no meeting sides in distant straightness.

Many have travelled before in North Wales. English travellers who came over the Border with the spirit of adventure into a foreign land. On foot, on horseback, and in creaking coach and rolling carriage. Coming into this land of mountains and quick streams, of mean inns and uncouth natives. And of rain, and always damp beds. A land of horse fairs and harpists.

Many have been the travellers in North Wales. The witty Mr. Hucks, B.A. in 1795, Giraldus Cambrensis in 1188, and the gentlemanly John Byng, author of *The Torrington Diaries*, who travelled in 1784 and 1787. The classic tours of Pennant in 1770 to 1776. And Dr. Johnson, in mortal terror of the precipices and the roads, in 1774. Defoe, in 1724, making his tour through the Isle of Britain, and Rowlandson, the artist, who made a series of sketches of his tour in North Wales which he made with Henry Wigstead in 1797. And the moderns, starting with Borrow in 1854.

They suffered, these early travellers. Poor Hucks at Welshpool in Montgomeryshire: ". . . the road from thence to Llanfyllin is very intricate, and we contrived to lose our way more than once, notwithstanding that we had been told that it was as straight as an arrow. It was late when we arrived . . . could get nothing but dry bread and bad cheese, poor cheer for two hungry travellers that had scarcely eaten anything since breakfast."

And Byng: "Here began a specimen of Welsh dirt; for my blankets stank so intolerably that I was obliged to use a quarter of brandy to sweeten them." This was Montgomery town.

Wild Wales indeed, and only the fascinating desolation of the place for compensation. Mountains, sleeping monsters, with a thousand graves around, and Arthur himself buried somewhere perhaps in the heart of the old rock. The moors and the bogs where, in daytime, the curlew call and the snipe flash shyly away, and only in moonshine do the fairies dance, the witches ride.

The Border of England and Wales a place for the churchy. Folklore and fairies.

For a long time the fairies have lived with the Welsh. And perhaps with a greater love for the north of the country. Where there are none of the great cities of the industrial south. For it is well known that the Little People do not like the touch of iron. And no fairy would stay long in the tinplate works and in the foundries.

But the mountains and lakes and the bogs of the North are the places which the Little Folk haunt now. Coming sometimes to the upland farms, or seen by some late traveller in the moonlight.

The legends and the stories remain. And at heart most of the Northern Welsh believe in fairies. Perhaps not the landladies of the seaside boarding-houses or the snob wives of the little towns. But the people best to know and best to understand; the women of the farms and the cottages; they speak still of what happened to mother, of the tale that granny told before she died as she looked out through the dark window. Often they tell of what has happened to themselves, half ashamed of the memory from some long-gone year.

I shall always remember the railwayman. It was one of those sad November days when the last brown leaves flutter against window panes and rattle in the wind on the doorstep. When the lamps are lit early at four in the afternoon. For I still have to trim a wick and strike a match and every week tilt paraffin. And when there are mists in the mornings and the papers tell of dark, dirty fog in the cities, of buses slow, and how trains travel to an explosion and dipping signals rear useless in the gloom.

A November day on the Welsh Border with the leaves on lawn and drive, and twig brooms and a smouldering bonfire in the corner of the garden before the old rustic summerhouse. A little wind, too, up from the English plain, the cold wind from the east which bends the tops of the conifer coppice. A wind which brings the noise of a distant ploughing, a tractor clear, and then lost again until the next stir of air comes. And only the fast-turning earth, shining brown across the flat English fields, sign of the winter ploughing.

A November day with the cows waiting heads to cowhouse door. The hay full in the cratch and the hens in great drooping groups tight against the hay in the stackyards.

And I bowling the barrow of old leaves. Golden brown of the beeches and the triangular forms of the chestnuts. With sometimes the graduated yellows of oaks and ash, gay and golden among the deader leaves. Bowling the leaves to the bonfire by the rustic summerhouse. A piled-high bonfire with a great, lazy column of smoke, leaning away only when the wind comes. And sometimes a lick of flame as the air moves, is still again.

Then the rattle of the drive gate. A lift and a ping as the fancy latch opens. After that the pendulum clicking of the gate as it swings in and out on its black, greased hinges.

He was coming across the lawn, his pointed best shoes long and flopping on the grass. His uniformed trousers clipped at the ankles and his hands cupped to his mouth, he blowing with an owl of a whistle into a hole between his palms. The railway company's markings fresh and new on the lapels of his coat.

He came right over to me and held his hands flat over the smoking leaves. The fingers splayed out and bending in and out to his palms. Then a smack together and he put them deep and finally in his trousers pockets.

Staring into the black and brown bonfire, he told me that she had died that morning, his little girl with the black-ribboned plaits and the cheeky answer. Told me that the disease had carried her off at last. The pneumonia which had flared up into tubercular lungs. They had taken her away to the mountains to the sanatorium; the school doctor had been wonderfully kind to arrange all that. But a month ago they had brought her home again.

She had died last night; he had the certificate in his pocket. He pressed the inside of his elbow hard against his coat, and then told me.

She had been six. A wonderful age for the Little Folk. She had had a little bed in the front parlour. There where she could see the narrow patch of lawn in front of the cottage, the green privet hedge and across the lane to the little beech wood. He told me how she had loved to watch out from her bed; we had to raise her up on pillows, he said. How she would watch out through the window, and in the last days had been always looking out at the wood, so that they could hardly bear to get her to turn her eyes to them when they came in the room. And during the nights when they sat up with her, she hardly seemed to sleep, ever. But was watching the black night beyond the window panes. Whispering to ask them not to draw the curtains and to keep the lamp down low. They did that, for that was what she wanted, and they wanted her to go happily.

Last night she had gone. They came out of the beech wood to fetch her, he said.

Did you see them?

Only heard their tinkling laughter as they danced in the lane. But Gwen had heard them all right, for she was smiling. Mam and me stood one each side of the bed looking down at her, sometimes. And sometimes out to the night and the lane beyond the window. The missus and me were a bit frightened, a bit happy, too, wondering if they'd come right up to the window, into the room, maybe. But when we heard them calling, we knew that it would be Gwen who would have to go out to them. They knew her name all right. And she went out to them easily and happily.

I raked the edge of the bonfire with my twig broom. Tipped on more dead leaves to the smoking heap. Tightened my jacket around me, for the wind from the east was stronger and colder, rattling the bare twigs in the hedges and rustling the old box hedges around the garden walks.

Oh, I said, are you sure?

Sure? Sure indeed. We're not lonely either, for she's only changed homes, that's all. Gone across the lane to live in the beech wood, and they'll look after her there.

This is the beginning of my journey, the first land of my own country. Here in the Border and the Paradise country; for here is Powisland, the Paradise of Wales. Here was the old kingdom of a Welsh prince, and still the sweetest country in the land.

Ear to the ground in Montgomeryshire, Denbighshire. A mile from England and hear all the coming and going. Legions and the running feet, full moon or the dark night. Plough the land with fast-moving tractor, glean the coins, the broken cup.

A quiet, gentle land. With only the ridge on the hill to show the defence. All the graves deep and hidden and forgotten far away.

I start in England. For the Border is wide and Wales reaches into England and the English stretch into Wales. There is a constant coming and going, and sometimes those from the other land make a new home. Many of the Border villages have the Welsh names, but the English have come, for ever. The garage and the post office and the inns are English. But still the chapels sing sweet Welsh hymns on Sunday. The Welsh names, Hughes and Jones and Thomas. And the stranger names, Broom, Jehu and Gittings.

Once a week, from the mountain and the valley farms, comes the trip to market.

The market towns of North Wales have the same quiet sleepiness all days of the week except one. And on market day a new life comes. A bustle, and the empty steel pens of the Smithfield fill with cattle and sheep and calves. Auctioneers with the loud voices and fast-banging sticks. Shops with the constant customers. Lilt of Welsh, and the second time of asking in English. Ring of tills and the town road-sweeper wears a peaked cap and takes in the sixpences for the parked cars. Or the cap has the white words *Market Inspector* or *Smithfield Inspector*.

Dolgelley dull under the shadow of Cader Idris. And in sweet, full-foliaged mid-Wales, there in the richness of the land of Powys, quiet Welshpool, a safe mile from the flooding Severn. And still in rich mid-Wales, Llanidloes and Machynlleth. Or up to the wonderful island, Llangefni in the mists of Anglesey. Or St. Asaph village, a sleeping city with its cathedral. Llangollen sweet on the Dee, with its memory of the Ladies Bohemian. Harlech with its castle, giddy and mountain-high above the golf course, marbles before the sea.

The market towns where yet the noise of horse and trap. High-stepping and the quick clap of hoofs. Leather harness scrubbed and oiled and made satin black for market day. Glint of polished brass and in the winter the sparks of ice nails, put specially in, horse-shoes with the large-headed nails for the icy roads. Cars and the trailers piled high with eggs and the gutted rabbits. Blue-redness of dressed chickens, gay with the bright green of parsley. Plums with the dull autumn bloom. Snowdrops tied with tape, dainty for Easter. Baskets of apples, sweet, and the big green cookers. Richness of the valleys coming in to Welshpool and Newtown and Machynlleth. Into Caernarvon and Llanrwst. Away, away in indecent haste, labelled and boxed in vans and lorries. Fast into England. Train-loads of cattle, red against the bars, wild-eyed, drip-nosed.

Oswestry is a main market town of the Border country. And at Oswestry was born the poet Wilfred Owen. His father, Tom Owen, was on the staff of the G.W.R. and later became station-master at Shrewsbury and Birkenhead. Also something of a sportsman, Owen's father, and was interested in local football and cricket. His mother was a daughter of an ex-mayor of the town, an Alderman Shaw who was in business as an ironmonger. Owen was born at Plas Wilmot and his godmother was a Miss Jane Parry.

Oswestry is in England, in proud, flat Shropshire, land of Mary

16

Webb. But the town is only a few miles from Wales, and on market day the people from the valleys and the mountains come into Oswestry in bus and car and with horse and trap. The streets are talked with the Welsh language, and only in the markets are the crafty English. Men from Lancashire and the Potteries who come to buy and to take away to hungry cities.

Oswestry, though in Shropshire, belongs to the Welsh on market Wednesday. And although the English farmers come they pass unnoticed in smart riding mac and brown breeches, talking their English freely in shop and Smithfield.

Only the Welsh people stand in the groups on the streets. The chat, the market-day talk. Seeing Mrs. Pryce every day of the week, perhaps in the village or on the next farm, but meeting her in town and there must be the talk, the price of hens and the fantastic low of butter. And others join in, with best black dresses and strong shopping bags and great yellow empty egg and butter baskets. Join in and talk and gossip on the pavements. With the sharp corners of the baskets poking the passers-by, and making prams tilt in the air to pass. So the policeman comes, polite, and they have to move. With loath last words and a mocking smile.

A great day for the shopkeepers. The streets are grey and quiet in the first two hours. Only the cattle coming in frightened, jostling heaps, with the low heads and the whacking hazel sticks of the urging drovers. Or the sheep, anxious and obedient and aching for the quiet of the pens.

Come the first cars, the first shoppers to fill bag and basket before the crowd comes. In the produce market the stallholders set up stacks of empty baskets and hanging, hungry scales for the eggs and the poultry and the summer fruit and the winter greens.

Up in the Smithfield the pens are filling with fat lambs and bleating mother-lost calves. Store pigs and sows with litters. Bulls chained and docile to long, concrete-sunk bars. Heifers and barren cows and store cattle and cows in calf and milkers, red and white, white and black, in the high steel pens. Bullocks and dressed rams. Rams made Beau Brummell for the sale. Heads clean and the wool of the back made a beauty colour of deep orange and faint yellow. This powder rubbed into the backs, and tails are trimmed neat and the whole ram a smart, spruced gentleman. The extra guineas for the extra care.

Soon in the Smithfield the bells begin to ring. The sharp clang of the handbells waved furious by auctioneer's man. A pause sometimes as the smooth handle is changed from hand to hand. Or the louder noise of the polished brass bells on a stand and rung by a short piece of rope.

The auctions start. The penned sheep and pigs sold in their pens by the auctioneer moving from place to place on a narrow wooden planking. His clerk by his side with the numbers entered and the price of the sale written up quick in pencil.

The cows and the heifers and the calves have the red numbers pasted on. And they are driven into a sale ring, and there sold by bamboo-sticked auctioneers. Only the bulls, sullen and blowing, are sold in their places.

Comes the late afternoon. The livestock lorries are loaded up to drive away to farm or city. And down in the railway cattle yards they pen the stock.

In the shops the worried, persistent crowd of buyers thins out, and the till drawers spring out only once in a while. Floors are swept and the dropped litter is taken out to the pavement and the gutter. There blown away by some country wind come in to market. The countrymen speed home for Wales and late tea, the change to old clothes and the evening milking.

Rivers flow towards the Border, and their valleys are the roads into Wales, the ways to the heart of my country. The Severn and the Dee, romantic rivers of the Gateway to Wales.

The Severn down from Plinlimmon, in a great needless hurry. So that in the Border they have taken away all its trees and the banks are bare and naked. The waters will flow quickly down to the Bristol Channel, not stay to soak Maesbury and Pool Quay. An ugly river and thin, with quick whirlpools and deep quiet black pools, white foam drifting slow.

The Dee, lovely from Bala Lake and tumbling white and rainbow spray through Llangollen. On to Chester and the sea. Factories of the North-West Wales tippling in their waste.

But there are the other rivers on the Border. The Vyrnwy and the Tanat. Trout in plenty and ugly-jawed pike in the deep reaches above the quiet ivy-covered mills.

I was born a few fields away from the last slow waters of the Vyrnwy. The river runs snugly into the Severn at Llanymynech. The two waters joining quietly with only a little sideways flow of current, shy for a moment and then the great slow sweep on to the sea.

The Vyrnwy is let loose from Lake Vyrnwy. The fixed amount from the Act of Parliament lake. Blue in the mountain sunshine and wonderfully pretty. With the thousand acres of larch and fir and pine. Making sharp sighing music when the wind blows, but the singing trees look down on a buried valley. There, where a church crumbles and the old sad houses of Llanwydden stay for ever under the water. And when the summer is dry and the streams from the mountains are slow, and when in Liverpool they put notices in the paper to say that the water is precious and waste not for pavements or the washing of cars, then the old people look out across the waters. Hoping that a grey stone may proudly show or moss-covered slate catch the moonlight. But the water is deep and with the rains of autumn deeper will the gauges read. And the grey pavements of Liverpool will be wet in the early morning again. And the ships sail out with the Welsh water sweet and with the price paid. Acts of Parliament and full compensation. The old people are dying and bitterness is almost forgotten. The young with good jobs, and progress and broken hearts two a penny always.

The river flows through the hills, lonely. With an angler sometimes finding this lovely river. A place for rising trout where the river bed shelves and the water flows with an annoyed ripple. Flicking out sunlight and throwing up the dancing reflected light yellow on the underside of the leaning willows and the dark-greened alders. Surge of water against the mossy boulders and a rattle in the roots of some tree, the earth washed away by a winter flood.

The shallows where once the fords were and the pack-horses crossed, or where the stepping-stones reached out neat and regular and tidy. Spaces now in the old stones, where some tree has come down in flood and the stones have been moved. And no Lord of the Manor or land-owning squire to see that the stones are straightened again. The Parish Council does not care and the bridge around the bend is made of best concrete and the girders have been tested for stress and strain, are rustproof and almost everlasting.

Deep pools, too, where the current hardly moves. And a yellow leaf twisting down with whirring stalk settles still on the water. Only in midstream is the gentle current. All the fallen leaves are yellow and brown on the edge of the pool. Only the hurried swim of a water rat or the anxious pushing of a water-hen or jerking coot.

These deep, serene pools in the quiet North Wales rivers. Only once in the years the boat passing, and then some new toy of village parson or at-home schoolboy. No well-kept walks on the banks and reaches where no rod has ever spun for the big-bodied pike. Once or twice in the twelvemonth the farmer comes and stands on his river bank, looking through the barbed-wire fencing. Or perhaps harvest time and the tea is eaten in the shade of some big tree on the edge of the river. And from the coolness the slops of tea are splashed into the river, or a hard crust sent floating away. Or at ploughing time a pausing of the tractor and a re-arranging of the folded meal sack on the hard iron seat. A stretch of the legs, lit cigarette, and the flaming match spun into the river. A hiss and the white wood quiet on the water.

Deep pools where the river bends and the fields are eaten away with river depth. The gravel adding to a wide grey stony shore on the other side. Land taken from one parish and added crumbs at a time to another boundary. One farm feet gained in gravel shore, and the losing farm plants the willow piles and weaves in the supple saplings. Fills in behind with earth and caps with large stones. For the hope is that the willow will grow and make a stout new home for itself. Be stronger than the river and tougher than concrete bags or great stone walls.

And along the rivers there are the mills. Mostly quiet now, but the pools are deep behind the stone dams.

Meifod is a village on the Vyrnwy, close to the old home of the princes of Powisland. Near here, too, is Dolobran, home of the Quaker Lloyds. And between Meifod and Llansantffraid is the mound in a bend of the Vyrnwy where Owain de Galles had his great home at Plas-yn-Dinas. He who so hated the English that he went to France to fight against them. But his Welsh squire assassinated him when they were out together. And the squire went joyfully with news of what he had done, went joyfully to the English commander. And was sadly, sternly rebuked for what he had done. So died Owain de Galles, great Welshman. His home is now only a place of grassy earthworks, with the river still in a half-circle protecting it. I have stood there on the mounds in the mellow autumn sunshine and quietness. And the only near house a farm, hidden behind trees and with only blue tea-time smoke curling above the wood. Stood there, remembering the great wooden house which was once on this mound. Full of comings and goings, water fetched, and the messengers with news of battle and of gossip.

Llansantffraid and the house where I was born. With old Georgian windows viewing a great slope of hillside, green always with pines and firs. Black at night and deadly alive with the anxious hoots of owls, the cackling crows of the cock pheasants. A wood which held all mystery for me and the twilight and the trees never a land to explore, never a place to wander in, even in August sunshine. A wood which made the mournful noises when the east wind came cold. And a fantastic swaying and bough shaking when the west wind came with its rain and echo in the old chimney-pots.

A lawn, a brook, and a great weeping willow tree. Walnut trees high and wide and every year rich with nut. The one corner of the garden with a Douglas fir, fighting the ivy to reach the sky. And a great orchard of sweet and cookers, of pear and plum, of ladders and men picking and reaching.

Just below Llansantffraid is Clawdd Coch, where was the Roman station, Mediolanum. Just above here is a curved ridge, where some glacier stopped in the Ice Age. The earth is sand and rounded pebble and a wonderful home for rabbits. The soil loose and easy to warren. Deep holes with the kicked-out yellow earth and the smaller grass-covered bolt-holes. Here come the rabbit catchers with spades and ugly steel traps set overnight. Or here come the Saturday-afternoon men from the village, with ferrets and loose nets. Placing the nets over the holes and then sending in the supple, sniffing, pink-nosed ferret on the end of a long, stout cord. The ferret starved for a day and eager for the hunt. The rabbits run and are caught in the nets. Quickly killed with strong, hard hands, neck broken and the watch again. A Saturday-afternoon sport with the farmer having half the money from the sale of the rabbit to the produce merchants. But the warrens are big and sometimes the ferrets are lazy. And sunset and the first morning light bring out the uncaught rabbits. Hopping and cautious to nibble hazel stems and tender grass. White tails ready to bob for danger and every smell and noise on the wind a pause from feeding.

Before the Vyrnwy joins the Severn it is itself joined by the Tanat and the Cain.

The Cain is a lonely valley of good farms and gentle-sided hills. And Wales starts proper with the rise to the foothills. There the black hair and the high cheekbones. Llanfyllin, and the Welsh spoken in the streets. Pubs and inns and the hotels are only for the English, in search of health and beauty and the farm butter melting ready on the tongue.

The Cain, small dainty river, comes through from Llanfyllin, small market town with the lovely old red of its brick church. In the old days famous for its strong beer, and the fondness for it of its people. And a fondness, too, for fire, chapel and Town Hall once going in smoke and flame. But sleepy enough now, with most of the market trade taken away by car and train to Oswestry. A place to talk in, Llanfyllin, to argue and discuss. With always the standers in the streets. And on market day the sober clumps of people. Men in dark suits and young lads in creased blue serge with the staid hats. Deaf to the horns of passing cars, the shouts, the gloved fist. Bumper to the knees with gentle rub and the sharp look round before the step aside. A word as the car passes, the old English. I narrow the wide, arty knot to my tie, drive on.

Mystics come and go, still with the strange fire in the quiet villages and lonely mountain farms. With knowledge unlocked gently in the yellow of two burner paraffin lamps, thought and the county library. Sermons made by lay preachers towards midnight. Read out with all the fire on a Sunday.

Above Llanfyllin, near Lake Vyrnwy, steep in the hills, the farm of Dolwar Fechain, where Ann Griffiths was born. Dying young and in her few years writing only seventy-five verses of glorious hymns. Treasured now as the sweetest in the Welsh language, full of wonder and mysticism. They have built her a chapel to remember her. And her face full of beauty and tenderness and her mouth gentle and sad looks down in effigy.

In the valley of the Tanat is Llanrhaiadr yn Mochnant, with its rush of waterfall, 210 feet high. Once the vicar here was Dr. William Morgan, famous as the first translator of the Bible into Welsh and who later became Bishop of Llandaff and of St. Asaph. In this valley, too, is Llangynog, in shadow of the Berwyn mountains, the grand boundary of Merioneth county and Montgomeryshire here.

The bleak Berwyn mountains with the Pennant glen, famous as a haunt of the fairies. And the Hounds of Hell haunt and hunt these mountains. The Devil is their huntsman and the hounds are bright red and as they hunt in the air they drop blood to the slopes beneath. On certain nights they hunt, this frightful pack, meeting at some cross-roads and waiting there until Satan comes. And they chase the souls of the newly departed, those who in the days and nights before have died. Their souls have been sent to the bleak slopes of the Berwyns to wait, those who are damned. And there they have to stay until the hounds come with their ghastly bay and their master riding high in the sky behind them. They come with cry and glee to drive the unhappy souls to their appointed places in hell.

The Hounds of Hell still haunt; any night Satan may meet his pack at cross-roads on some mountain slope. People have seen the Hounds in full cry across a low sky. Mountain farmers have heard the awful baying, the once-heard sound of a lifetime. On wild nights late travellers pedal fast, and in the cars the eyes blink and watch as the road unfolds in the headlamps. And when people in the valleys die, and dogs bay to the moon, or whine in courtship through the night, then it is because they can see the Hounds gathering, or hear their calling from the mountains.

Not with the best of gay companions would I hike over the Berwyns at night when the wind is high and the rain hisses from the tops of the rocky places. For I know and remember the tales which have been told me as I grew up. Of the girl who was chased by the Hounds and who saved herself by gathering the stones as she ran. Picking up clumps of rock and broken-away pieces of the mountain. She running on with these and only stopping when she had enough to make the shape of a rough cross on the hillside. And she lay there, crucified and safe and still, until the light of the new day came, and the Hounds faded away.

No one tells of having seen the Huntsman. But all know that he must be there, calling on his Hounds and never relenting until all the lost ones are in their appointed, dreadful places.

Ever there is the feel of the supernatural which the chapels have never been able to dissolve away. Rather with their talk of hell fire and damnation, still the theme of the older preachers, such talk of the unknown is made more real, more to be believed in.

But the old fun of pain is no more. The older amusements disappeared with the puritanical hatred of the chapels of the last century for any sort of trivial, worldly pleasure. No last lingering on of cock-fighting; the cock-pits are grassy now, and the cows graze quiet where once the blood-stained spur flashed and the lost feathers whirled. And only black crows walk in their perky, wobbling way across the quiet field, once noisy with afternoon spectators, arguments of better bird, shouts for a better cock.

Once, in my village, the old, very old, man tells me of the game of his youth. An old man who sits all the winter in a hard oak chair by the fire. And who, all the summer, sits on a bench outside his son's home in the sunshine. There with a great trail of rambler roses over his head, reaching high up to the tiny bedroom window. And summer and winter a stick in between his knees, the curved handle of it polished in his hand. His face with the brown wrinkles of old, much-heated china. By his ears, towards his chin, are thick white locks, the hair always clean, dazzling white in the sunshine.

In his slow, halting, spitting way he has told me many things. When he was wagoner on the farm and carried lime from the kilns three days' journey away. And of the days when moving the threshing machine, farm to farm, was the event of the month, with straining horses and wooden wedges under the wheels of the portable steam boiler. And when timber was carried always on timber wagons, pulled and loaded by horses. Days of many horse teams and long wooden timber wagons creaking along the road, where now the steel-built, rubber-tyred trailers spin quietly behind the cabbed tractors. Timber-felling in the old days when the only reason was patriotic. Beams and timbers from the Welsh valley estates going out to sea in the sailing-ships. No tree-felling at the death in the family, as is the way with the paupered county families now remaining. All the trees to pay the death duties. A great heaving of tractors, ploughing up the good pastured land with a great tear, a great churn up of the land into a muddy lane from the wood to the main road, a deep-rutted ugly scar.

And it was this old man who told me of a great game in the village, held in secret yet all knowing. How, on the public holidays, they had the fun of hen hitting, all the young men in the

village taking part. An ugly game, a blood-sport of the golf variety.

A hen taken and buried in the ground with only the inches of her neck and head showing. And the game, the great game, was to knock her head off with a stout club-ended stick. Drawing lots for the turns of hitting and the man to finally knock away the head declared the winner.

The old man knocked the bones of his knees with the palms of his hands as he told me the story. Gleefully and with the wrinkles in his face deeper and kinder. There in the sunlight outside the house, the brown stick between his knees, and over his head a whole great tree of rambler roses.

Montgomeryshire is a gentle county of river valleys and apple-tart mountains. On the east the Border county with England, and on the west rising to the inland mountain ranges. Smooth and lush in the valley farmlands and the foothills of the east. But moorland rugged further into Wales. With mountain farms and sheep walks, heather and gorse and brown peaty soil.

The Severn moves slow out of Wales at Llandrinio, where once the church tower was cracked with ghost-laying. Naked banks and the deep, dark pools with the sudden swirling twists of water. With foam edging the banks at the quiet sides of the corners, breaking away sometimes and sailing light, washing-day white downstream.

The cattle drink at the gravelled watering-places. Making earth paths down to the water with the years. Nose in the water and a roving, anxious eye for the fast-darting pike. For here, from the dark Severn pools they come, snapping down the black fluff chicks of the moorhen and a dart for the soft-fleshed nose of drinking cattle.

The Severn is the longest river in Britain and rising on the borders of Cardiganshire and Merionethshire. A trickle and a noisy little brook, anxious and fast in the beginning. And at the end the great drawling waterway of the West of England.

Sabrina, of Milton's *Comus*, was thrown into the water by her step-dame, Gwendolen, from a river meadow of the Severn. But "the water nymphs that in the bottom played, held up their pearled wrists and took her in". The meadow is at Abermule, where the Mule river from the Kerry hills joins the Severn. Still they call the field Dolforwyn, The Maid's Meadow. Sabrina who gave her name to the Severn.

The river winds sleepy up from the Border to Pool Quay, a quiet place with a view across the valley to the heights of Breidden Hill. This hill with the pointed column on the top, remembering Admiral Rodney and his ships in particular. Wooden walls of England made from the oaks of the Border country. And the land-owning gentry gave him the monument, a needle black in a great green and grey cushion.

The land of the Severn valley is all the way fertile. The farms well kept and rich. The fields grass-green and yellow with wheat and oats and barley. The tractors give out the chug-chug and the sudden spurts of black exhaust smoke. All up the Severn valley are the good herds of cows, pedigree and tested. With Wessex pigs rooting in the fields after harvest time, and bright milk churns on stands, outside the farm gates. The farmers are breeched and prosperous. Their cars large and their farms well managed. Farm is their business and no scratching a hard living from a bare farm of the barren mountains. The root crops flourish and are stored away in long dumps in the fields, safe from the winter frost under many layers of straw. And the only danger the rats which might burrow with the winter frosts.

I meet the great milk lorries heading east to England. Either the many racks of metal churns in clanking rows or the big white tankers, hurrying with the Severn valley milk to the Midlands. Babies in the sooty cities and milk for the cups of char, milk for the invalids and noisy-drinking children in the schools.

The stock reared here, too, bullocks fed and fattened on meal and graded and taken blissful away to the abattoirs.

The horse teams are leaving; most of the farms have the tractors now. Cheaper and less trouble. No vet's bills, and spare parts from the market town make the machine work again.

But the great farm horse is still kept. A one or a two on many farms. Useful at the harvest time and for the odd jobs. The days of fancy harness and proud wagoners left for the hill farmers now. The conservative ones who have not a great love for petrol and things which explode with a hot pipeful of tobacco.

The richness of the river valley. The old monks loved it, building their Cistercian abbeys in the well-watered gentle places. One at Pool Quay, Strata Marcella, on the edge of the Severn, with the views up to the mountains, and far down to the great flat plain of Shropshire. The abbey quite gone now and only awkward grassy mounds and level green lawns left. Once the sweet chanting and the husbandry and the fish on Friday. But now the cars race by on the main good road and only the slope to remember what once lay below in the sweet meadow by the Severn. The rise in the road is still Abbey Bank.

On the road to Welshpool is Buttington. History here for the asking. For it was as far as here that the Danes reached in the time of Alfred the Great. Here, too, at Rhyd-y-groes the Mercians were defeated by the Welsh Gruffydd ap Llewelyn. And of Rhyd-y-groes the Mabinogion, those strange tales from the ancient Welsh, tell how Arthur crossed here. And in later times the barges came upstream to Pool Quay, and commerce and travel was on the slow way of the Severn.

Something of a nuisance the Severn. The waters after rain time flood fast, and from Welshpool to the Border and beyond a danger always of yellow water high to the stacks and staining the downstairs rooms. Leaving mud on the floors and the land wet and soggy. Hay wetted, and the corn in the ricks made mouldy.

Coming towards me an old, untidy, snorting lorry. Old green paint and a high yellow-white load. Small cut, certain shaped, pieces of timber. Looking up, I knew the patterns of the wood; this was a clogger's load on the way to the railway station.

The clogger has a tent by the river. Not the waterproof green of the camper, with a cylinder of portable gas at the back, bottled city comfort. Not the patched tent of old tarpaulin, sagging, and the edges held down by heavy stones, outhouse of the gipsy caravan.

But a grey thing, a round bell tent. Bought cheap after the First World War and the numbers still black on an inside flap.

This tent set up by some small river where the alders grow thick. A bargain has been made with the owner of the land. A bargain for all the standing trees on the river bank. This arranged, perhaps, two years in advance on a half-day's cycling.

The clogger has lodgings in some near village. And every day comes to the river bank to work. A skilled job, making wooden soles for clogs. Felling alder trees and stripping the bark, sawing up the wood into short lengths. And after that using a special tool and cutting the wood into the rough shape of the finished sole. Stacking these in neat heaps, white and symmetrical. And a day coming every few months when the clog bottoms are taken to the railway station and sent away to the manufacturers. A livestock lorry hired, or perhaps the coal lorry from the station yard, all the coal dust swept away and sacks laid on the floor. Then the white wooden soles are stacked and carted to the waiting truck.

In the fine weather the clogger works at tree-felling and at bark stripping, and at sawing up the trunks into the short, measured lengths. And he stores these just inside the dark tent. Ready for the wet weather and the sitting on a small stool at the V-shaped entrance, using a small old log for a stool and heated by a small paraffin stove. Trimming and cutting the log lengths to the proper shape. Ready for distant mill or distant mine, for clatter of clogs on street paving, loud and early morning, or at the end of a shift with a drag of feet.

Out of Buttington I heard the squealing. Distant and high pitched, ending suddenly with a faint, lasting echo over the green and the ploughed fields.

On some farm, then, was the pig-killing.

An event of the twelvemonth is the pig-killing. All the mountain and the lowland farms kill one or two pigs in the year.

A pig is held back at the time of selling of the young ones. Is kept back and in the growing time is left to wander about the yards and woods. Rooting for choice herbs and wallowing in the mud of the pools. Lying in the sunshine and sleeping in the sty at the end of the farm buildings. A warm place of straw floor and snug corners, for pigs are clean and careful animals.

And one day, perhaps, is done the ringing. This if the pig roots too much and turns over much good land. A brass ring is fixed through the nose with a special semicircular-ended pliers. The ring held open in the mouth of the pliers and the pig held by a farm-hand. Then a quick grasp of the black plier handles and the ring is closed in the snout of the pig. A squeal and a kick, and a good-natured slap on its back. The urge to prod and push in the ground is still there, but each touch of the ring on the earth will cause pain. The yards and the meadowlands are safe. The brass ring shines ornamental in the sunlight, a flash with every ear-flapping shake of the head against the summer flies.

On the smaller farms it is the wife who does the actual ringing while her husband and perhaps the son, Saturday home from school, hold the pig. The woman with her coarse, worked hands, the lines of the years black in the cracks. She who helps in the harvest, and can carry on with the lambing when her husband is down with the 'flu.

Then one morning after months of freedom the door of the little yard in front of the pig-sty is closed. From now on it will be the fattening. No more roaming and a search for the titbits. But night and morning now the bucket of pigs' food is brought. Meal and special fattening foods made hot and steaming and tasty with hot water, and perhaps a handful of white flour. All stirred into a thick gruel with a flat piece of board. Taken to the sty. The pig knows the clank of bucket handle and squeals at the door. A pushing up of the snout and a tapping with the stirring board as the man comes in. The bucket is tilted and the food is slopped into a narrow iron trough. And as the pig slobbers up the meal the farmer leans over and scratches the white, coarse-haired back with blunt finger-nails.

The pig is fatted and the killing day comes. Sometimes it is done by the village butcher on his half-day or by a travelling farm butcher who goes from farm to farm to do the sheep- and pig-killing. He comes at a fixed hour and expects then to find the water boiling in the outside washhouse, and the bench laid ready in some convenient spot.

The butcher comes with his bag of tools greased and gleaming. A rope is placed in the ring of the pig and it is dragged by the snout to the yard, laid on the bench, and then the killing is done. The pig is opened up and then hung up whole by the hind legs in the back kitchen. With a little pudding bowl under the pegged-open mouth to catch the stray blood. Memories of my childhood when home from school in the darkness of winter's evening I would open the back door suddenly, forgetting that to-day had been the killing. Seeing the opened inside of the pig as it hung up, a notched piece of wood and a rope to the back legs to hold up the body to the steel hook on some cross-beam. A stare at the inside held apart by a long pointed stick, with the tasty offal dangling over it.

The pig hanging there for one or two days, depending on the weather, and then the butcher coming again to do the cutting up. The pig carried out stiff and straight to the outside and there cut up into hams and sides and fresh ribbed meat with quick rasps of little saws and curls of sharp knives. The body made neat and orderly and fit for tasty breakfast and late savoury supper by the relentless hands of the butcher. The one who used to come to my home was an efficient giant of a man with a great beard which seemed to get in the way of his words at the rare times when he spoke. Well I remember him with red blood spray splashed on to his beard and his huge body working in a sure certain way. He who walked always from farm to farm and who was most particular that the water should be scalding hot before he would start to scrape away the hairs.

Then after the cutting up comes the salting. Days and days of it. The hams and the sides basted with salt rubbed deep by pressing, circular-moving hands.

The fresh meat given away and savouries at every meal, and only from habit is the big black kettle put on, hot water ready for the pigs' food. But the sty is empty and the hens scratch in the straw and the stout wooden door swings back with every high wind.

In the kitchen the hams and bacon sides hang from the row of hooks found on the beams in every Welsh farmhouse kitchen. The white muslin has been sewn around the bacon and the ham. All waits for the slicing knife, for winter dinners and summer suppers.

Up the black Severn from Buttington and a safe half-mile from the quick-rising river is Welshpool. A market town and once the selling centre for the mid-Wales flannel trade. Sheep grazed in the Severn valley and there was in the mid-Wales towns a prosperous woollen industry, founded by Flemish weavers who settled in the county in the Middle Ages. The woollen work done in the homes

of the workers, and Welsh woollen goods were noted for quality. The Industrial Revolution coming and with it the setting up of mills at Newtown, once called the Leeds of Wales. But the good earth was green and the coal had to be carried. Yorkshire improved their methods and technique and now the Welsh flannel trade has quite gone. Some of the buildings have been taken over for light industry and the old firms' names painted out on the brick walls. The rain wears the paint thin, and as I walk past, the black square letters show vaguely through. An advert for a firm forgotten, a remembrance of a trade gone for ever. But all for the good, perhaps. No old dyes to sewer the river and no plans for green belt or garden city will worry the burgesses.

Through Welshpool straight and slow is the Shropshire Union Canal. Quiet and no gaudy barge to ruffle the weeds, sway the green scum. The long locks are empty, with only the trickle of water from height to height through the great leaking doors. The banks are grassy and only the bridges are well kept, with the loose mortar pointed, for the traffic still passes heavy above. Under the cool of the arches the condensed water drops and the moss clings green to quiet stone. Bramble twists across the water, ivy spears up the bridge walls. Once on the canal the lap of the wake, gentle from the long, slow barges. The horse pulling and the long tow-rope humming in the cold winds east from the English plain. This wind from the east, *wind from the feet of the dead* the Border people call it. A shrill, sharp wind, bringing blue to the nose and red chap to the hands.

The barges which were loaded with sand and lime and goods for the Border towns. Slow and sure transport before the railways came. With smoke from the cabin at the back of the boat and the door opening into the well under the steering handle. Polished and smooth and a hand always to keep the boat to the centre of the canal.

Families lived once on the canal and the barge was home. Summer, and the pause under the cool shadow of the bridge. Winter, and the ice and the ice-breaking boat out. Its steel-edged bow and the strong horses ploughing the night ice with crackle and groan. The ice left in uneven wobbling floes on the swaying water, a way clear for the barges and the canal open.

Now the last barge is gone and the last horse stabled, the polished harness sold to some farm. The brass with the company's proud letters on some milk-float now, or pulling some June hay-cart.

They built great warehouses along the edge of the canal for the barges to draw in to. With slated canopies so that the unloading could be done under cover. In some of the mid-Wales towns the firms use the warehouses for storage. In other places they are used to store hay or winter cattle. For the focal points have altered and new termini have come into being. Once some length of canal was a feeding point for a whole hinterland of countryside. The teams and the farm wagons coming down all the day and the bricks and the sand and the mortar and all the imported goods carried from the canal warehouse. An inn and a house for the warehouseman built. Stables and stalls for the horses.

The trade is gone and now the railway yards and the fleets of lorries distribute quickly the feeding-stuffs for cattle, the wireless set bought from the London store. And so the inn has become a house and the home of the warehouseman has become a small-holding. The canal that once brought gossip and news and the scandal of the moving home, now waters cattle. Splayed hoofs push the clayey bank to colour yellow the water. Only the cattle and the bus-loads of red-faced fishermen on a Sunday use the water. And the skaters and the boys when the hard frost comes and there are no crushing boats, no unbending steel to break the smoothness.

Out of Welshpool, up the main street and through the old upper part of the town. Houses with steps and black and white buildings.

On the road from Welshpool over the banks, wooded land and farms and the rolling fields. Here at Broniarth Hill the Lollard, Sir John Oldcastle, a great leader of English Nonconformity, was captured by Edward de Cherleton, Lord of Powys, in 1417. A man fond of persecution was de Cherleton and one of the particular enemies of Owain Glyndwr.

A winter's morning as I passed Broniarth Hill. A coolness in the air and the sun behind great snow clouds, lighting golden their very edges. And on the quiet fields of the hill the cattle were eating kale, shaking the long green stalks and licking up the leaves. Sheep were pulling hay from a long feed trough, standing grey in neat rows. Hard to remember that here Oldcastle saw the end of his gallant four years of freedom.

This road runs across country from Welshpool to Llanfyllin. An up-and-down road with lanes and wide, hedged paths leading off it.

They who know the roads in the four seasons of tearing wind or tempting sunshine. All hands of time, darkness and light and the uneasy in-between.

Knowing every yard of every North Wales mile. The bends in the road, the forgotten wells, the certain hazel hedges where the certain straight, smooth sticks can every year be picked to be peeled and carved and twisted. All the roadside barns and the snug sheepfolds.

Not the hikers or the machine-legged cyclists. Or the man in the car with every mile watched for the flash of a milestone, the way mastered.

The tramps know the roads from Dolgelley to Bala and from Llanfyllin to Forden. These key towns, hubs for the homeless, the casual wards, once the Union workhouses.

Still they tramp up from England and across the Border counties. Up to Anglesey and back down the west coast to South Wales. A grand perambulation and every gentle house remembered. The

place where the hot water is certain. And the house where the
maids are trim and the gardener trips dainty behind a motor
mower and the master a prosperous belly and the brain addled
with intellectual progress. *Tramps to safe jobs* and never the bread
or the shrunken shirt. But always the offer of a job, to be the
third or the fourth gardener. A spade, and feet must walk the
same soil all day and never an urge to a distant horizon, the call
of a bend in the road.

Not on the main road will you meet the fairies, for the Little
People are not over keen on good macadam and A and B invitation to the first- and second-class roads. They rather know the old
tracks hedged in with great scrambling briars, black-berried and
with the hooks clinging to every passing trouser, making a ladder
glorious in every nylon. An enemy to the stray city walkers. These
lanes made for the cord farm breeches and the black wool stock-
ing. Made for those who go into the old lanes sometimes for the
stray animal or for the blackberries, soft and black and staining
hard hands red and crimson, making the nails gaudy and gay, a
Bond Street to wash off in the back kitchen with pumice and red
household soap. Those who go into the lane, the grass unused
track, for the nuts in the autumn. A shake of the hazel trees growing green on either side of the track. Long smooth brown stems
with the cool leaves and the nuts falling brown and stored in the
basket, kept ready for Christmas.

These old tracks, in the valleys down to the rivers. Crossing at
some old ford, the water there still shallow, the banks still sloping.
And the track lost again on the other side, the old paved way
ploughed under and only perhaps miles on the road seen again.

Or the Roman road wild across the top of the hills, straight, and
with a view, always.

Or walks around some old Hall turned farmhouse. A great
wilderness of a walled garden, but warm and snug and holding
the sunshine. Old pear trees trained long ago on the sunny south
walls, but straggling now. Or perhaps a vine, thick gnarled root
and heavy with fruit every year. Or perhaps in a corner a high
mulberry tree, remembrance of Jacobean days. The Hall now
with half its rooms empty and rats pawing and racing behind the
wainscoting. One wing of the house knocked down and the bricks
used to make the farm buildings, but the old foundations left white
across the yards. The Hall a farm now, with the family living
in a bunch of rooms at the one end of the house and the great oak
main staircase left bare and unused. Except, perhaps, at apple
time, when the barrow can be loaded and bowled into the once
merry main hall and a plank laid up the oak steps, and the winter

storage made easier that way. But in the run of days the back staircase only is used, that which once was used by the servants, a steep corridor of a place.

And around the Hall are perhaps walks where once were cool avenues. Tracks where the cattle stand now for shade in the summer, or backs to the rain in the winter. And only the arch of the hazel recalls what a lovely Elizabethan walk this must have been. The nut trees planted, and overhead the pliable stems joined and weaved together to form a growing arch, in shape to-day and in the summer a whole avenue of greenness.

Old mansions in the valleys and on the edge of the mountains. Time when the Vicar and the Squire were lords spiritual and temporal in the parish. Now the Vicarage is only half used, a dust and an echo in many rooms. And the maid-attics are lonely, plaster falling. Tithes now a matter of pounds and shillings, and I remember my father, staunch chapel man, angry always at having to make the cheque to the Church in Wales. He always waiting for the last demand, red with threat of court and Church militant.

The tithe barns are still to be seen in the various places. Now long ago sold to farmers and used to store hay or as a winter storm shelter for young cattle. Once the Church took the fixed amount of the crops and the barns were filled with parson's stock. The Church once owned the fields, too, the "glebe" fields, and the pasture next the house, from where I went, sad, only child, to school, was a "parson's field". And whenever on a dark winter's night we had to go to the village for the milk or for the evening post, then the saying was: "I'll come to send you as far as the end of the parson's field."

The Welsh parson is a force only in certain strongholds now. Nonconformity is divided into the many chapels, and most of the powerful public men are chapel deacons. Sitting each Sunday, starched-collared and black-suited, in the hard Big Seat just below the pulpit. Gods on show, and the hard, straight face lost only when the public praying comes.

Once on a Sunday comes the prayer meeting. Three or four take part. Going up to the front and giving out a hymn and after that on the knees on the red carpet to pray aloud. Sweet, romantic phrases and all the wild Celtic emotion, tender and loving, coming out in rich word, half song, half speech. A remembrance for all the ill in the world, every sinner, every place. And after it all a half-shamed rising, a brush with the folded, ironed hanky at the face wet with tears.

Outside Welshpool there is the great Powis Castle, the Castell Coch of Welsh history, the Red Castle.

Owned by the Herberts and with associations with Clive of India. One of its daughters was Lady Winifred Herbert, who became wife of the Jacobite Nithsdale and rescued him from the Tower of London in 1716.

Rounding a bend the colours came. Bright and harsh and sudden. With music and a movement of people. Parked cars in tidy rows with badged men setting them straight and orderly. This, then, must be a Show.

A great day, a holiday for the farmers from mountain and valley. All come down to the field made gay with the striped awnings of traders and with lines of bunting on the marquees. Banners on the main tent poles. Ice cream and lemonade and a tea tent with the canvas side open, and bickering at the tables between the sweating serving-women and the impatient farm lads. Impatient to be out on the field again and turning round to look out with half-raised slab cake and tea saucered for the quick cool.

Treasure hunts and filling of balloons. A competition to judge the weight of a fat lamb standing docile all day in a shaded pen.

And all the time a brass band playing. With a blare and a shine and wonderfully gay in braid and tunic and peaked caps.

Announcements are made from the loud-speakers, modern and

hoarse, on top of the wireless dealer's van. The events announced in Welsh and in English, and all with a great echo to them, unreal and not a bit like the real voice of Mr. Jones the auctioneer.

The Show day ends up with a dance. The modern young farmers dancing and the non-dancers staring through the hall doors, or making rude noises on the frosted lower window-panes.

A relaxation, the Show. And only a lesser day is the sheep-dog trials. This latter a slower business, with the dogs racing far up the field to bring the sheep down through posts and gateways to finally pen them in a three-sided stall. The dogs with the uncanny moving to master's whistle, the crouch to the shepherd's unspoken thought. Long-nosed, intelligent sheep-dogs with the brown, trusting eyes. And a whole job in life to order and control sheep, to rise and move, crouch and watch with ever an ear for the whistle of the master.

Sometimes to the small town or village comes the circus or fair. Tents rise, a circular roof for the ring, a Big Top where yesterday the cows grazed. And where to-morrow will be only the sawdust and the toffee papers and the empty cigarette cartons.

The fair with the central roundabout, rising and falling fierce dragons and green and yellow horses. Twirled brass poles in the naked electric lights, and the nimble-footed attendants dance to collect the coins. And around the main roundabout with its glass-fronted, snorting steam organ are the stalls. Where sober-suited Welsh lads roll pennies or take aim with shot-guns. Throw darts or hit the Test Your Strength with the mallet. These lads who can drive stakes with one hand into a pletching hedge, yet for them the bell at the top of the tall red stand will not ring. The trousered girl, woman of the fairs, clangs the bell every time with dainty hits of her many-ringed hand.

Shows and fairs and circuses, like the Eisteddfodau and the concerts, things to look forward to in the quiet villages of Wales. Where there can be no booking for plush stalls and the gods are an uneasy seat on a narrow back window ledge. Where the old magic of the theatre never comes. Those dying whisperings as the house lights fade, the long minutes of the interval before the curtain shivers and the last act comes.

On through the farmlands to Montgomery, the county town of Montgomeryshire, though now all the official business is divided between Welshpool and Newtown. Only a mile from England is Montgomery, and here is Offa's Dyke which runs from the Wye to Mold. A mound high in places, but often levelled and smooth. The Border country has two dykes, that of Offa and also Wat's Dyke, which runs from Maesbury in Shropshire up north to Holywell in Flintshire.

Here is Powisland, once a great province of the Welsh princes and taking in all of Montgomeryshire, Breconshire, Radnorshire and parts of Denbighshire. After the time of Offa, Shropshire, which once was also in the province, became a part of Mercia, and the Welsh princes left their home at Shrewsbury for Mathrafal, near Meifod, in the Vyrnwy valley.

Montgomeryshire reaches lush through Central Wales. Green and with the fields sometimes brown with the ploughing. Following behind are the crows, and nearer the sea the herring gulls.

Country farms where men rise early and work late. With milking and cattle feeding to be done Sunday and all week. With event and amusement slow, uncommercial things, village concerts and socials and dances.

On the Border dances and socials are held often, and a few a year in the market towns of the interior. The Young Farmers' Clubs and the Youth Organisations fix social evenings and dances. But the chapels do not approve of dancing and whist drives. Drinking and pleasures of the flesh are things of Satan. Drama, too, is a thing forbidden by the older deacons, though now the more progressive chapels have their own annual dramas with hired companies from South Wales as the star attraction.

The Eisteddfodau, these are things of culture and mind-broadening. Most districts have one or more Eisteddfodau in the year and often there are big area ones, too, such as that for the mid-Wales district, the Powis Eisteddfod. And, of course, there is the National Eisteddfod which is held in North and South Wales in alternate years.

The Eisteddfod is a competition for all music and arts and crafts. Choral and individual singing, reciting poetry, and handicrafts of all sorts. Money prizes always and the meetings continue always far past midnight. A chairman invited who is expected to give a substantial amount towards the funds and to make the shortest of speeches some time half-way through the meeting. And there is a *compère* who is called the conductor and who usually comes for the fun of the thing, with his expenses paid by the committee. The conductor must be a man of quick wit and fast joke and have a knack of getting order with an angry shake of his fist.

And at the Eisteddfod there is the penillion singing, that art

peculiar to the Welsh. The harp strumming one tune and the singer coming in on counterpoint. An old art and reviving strongly now. Not only penillion singing in the Eisteddfod competitions and in the concerts, but in the big kitchens of the mountain farms at the Noson Lawen. A kind of informal night with joke and impromptu songs. The harp the main instrument, the gilt of its frame twinkling in the firelight. Or shine steady in the straight glow of peat. The strings vibrating and the chords coming as it were from the great wide chimney with its view to the stars and the night outside sky. In the old days harp strings were made of black hair, but the old minstrel bards have gone now. The patron princes are sleeping, and who dare wander from place to place with harp and verse of praise? Who dare do that now and escape the law, the awkward question?

I go on to Newtown, where Robert Owen of Co-operative fame was born in 1771 and where he was buried in 1858. Once this town had much industry, when the flannel making was centralised here from the cottage homes of the workers.

On deeper into Wales, and there is Moat Lane Junction, where the line for South Wales branches. A clean, simple junction. Here stand the farmers on their way to and from the fairs and markets. Stand with the tips of their fingers in breeches pockets. And there is an old man with a paper carrier. One hand to the strings and the other gently underneath. For in there is a prize gander, white and cackling. Body safe deep in the brown paper and the head curving out, amazed and staring. Up and down the younger farmers walk, slapping bamboo sticks against brown leggings. And against the walls of the station lean the old farmers, looking across the rails and the platforms at the fields beyond. There perhaps where a whole family is picking potatoes, or land girls in green sweaters turn a potato riddle. Or where horses harrow a field or pull a fertiliser spreader.

This station with the very English name in the centre, almost, of Wales. Where in the summer, after the harvest, the farmers change for the trains to take them to Builth and Llandrindod Wells, the spas where they can rest, drink the waters and talk. With an aching back turned on the harvest and all the hay-lifting and stack-making,

And Llanidloes is near Moat Lane, the town which is fifteen miles only from the bare Plinlimmon top where starts the first waters of the Severn.

The land beyond Moat Lane and to the west changes. The uplands come and the streams are small and stony and noisy. Some of the richness goes from the land and there are acres where scrub grows, thorn and gorse and bracken. The road climbs and becomes hedgeless and the railway has an echo and a clatter in rocky cuttings, moss green and wet dripping. Sometimes the back of a small farmhouse is seen, a white child—face at the window—smear-nosed against the tiny panes. Or a lifeless chapel, weekday quiet, and grey stone built in a little coppice of conifers. Or the sudden whiteness of a cemetery on the slope of a mountainside. With sheep reaching through the iron railings to nibble the uncut grass, or perhaps a vision of black mourners, bare-headed, and crowded in one particular spot among the whiteness. And only the way the heads tilt back and the mouths open and slowly close to show that there is singing, the noise of the hymn lost in the clang and clatter of the train wheels. And staring away from the window I look up at the carriage photographs, of Devon and Cornwall, of stepped villages and crafty lobster pots. And when I look out again I see only mountains and hills, and streams which flow west now, west to the sea.

II. TO THE WEST AND THE SEA

TO THE WEST AND THE SEA

THE waters on the west side are lonely, Cardigan Bay stretching
blue and white away to Ireland. A few miles out there is the streak
of broken water which they call now Saint Patrick's Causeway.
And when the tides are very low this Causeway can be seen. A
relic of an ancient land out miles to where the sea now sweeps. A
land called Cantref-y-Gwaelod and taking in much of Cardigan
Bay.

Once the sailing-ships came in white and slow to Barmouth and
Portmadoc. And in those days the Causeway was Sarn Baddrwg,
the Evil Causeway. The ships wrecking there on this land where
now the sea shifts the sand each tide.

Barmouth and Portmadoc, Aberdovey and Towyn.

The strange long coast of Merionethshire, with the headlands
smooth and the great wide golden estuaries. The acres of sand
ridged with the ever-changing shapes. And when the tide is high,
blue in the summer sunshine, shimmering when the moon comes
up lantern-golden over Cader Idris.

The Dovey and the Mawddach. Little rivers from the mountains, opening out suddenly into great lonely estuaries. Harbours
once with the boats going out to Virginia. And the smugglers
creeping in quiet, the church vaults full of casks, heavy and still.
The tracks still across the hayfields to the tiny rocky coves. White,
empty crabs and the great flat stones, smooth with the waves from
every grinding tide.

Bells of Aberdovey. Listen on a windy night and you can hear
the soft, sweet, muted rings. Swing in the buried church with
fast-darting fishes quick in the moving bells. But when the wind
blows off the sea, all the strange sad noises come up from Cardigan

Bay. This is not the North Coast of the Wales with the resorts and the shacks and the camps gay with caravans. There only the memory of the spices carried once across Liverpool Bay come drifting in on the wind. Landing on the quiet dunes of Prestatyn, far from the bandstands and the quick-flashing sticks.

But here on the west side wait to see a mermaid combing her hair in the moonlight on some old black rock, made smooth and an easy seat by all the high tides of a thousand years. To see her with her graceful tail in the sea and the moon on her scales; catching the shine of her golden hair.

A mermaid combing her hair with a comb made smooth and strong of some old beautiful shell from a sandbank of the sea. For if you believe you can see anything in the moonlight between the Lleyn and Aberdovey, when the sea sways the long, glittering moon in the quiet waters. For these are lonely seas and only the small boats in the summer pass over the water. There are no sea lanes here, no ships passing every day with compass and look-out and all mechanical perfection. No great port to come into; now Portmadoc and Aberdovey and Barmouth receive only the stray ships, and there are no great long quays, and no high-dangling cranes or shunting yards with the engine bells clanging, or the echoing clank of buffer to buffer.

On Cardigan Bay, perhaps, the ghost ships sail. Old galleons of the Golden Age searching yet for adventure, for chase and treasure. And coming here with sail and poop. Ships of the Queen, or Spanish lost from the Armada and sailing ever round the coasts until all the watching came. And then slipping into Cardigan Bay to stay, for ever.

Mermaids and phantom ships, time and belief a shuttlecock. Hold and throw. Make time an age, and belief only the open inner eye.

I come to Machynlleth, come into this old town as I go west from mid-Wales. This market town on the Dovey where Owain Glyndwr held his Welsh Parliament in 1402. And where for me comes the first sniff of the sea, the knowledge of near salt water. Bleak heights and boggy lanes left behind. But still there can be the loneliness and desolation, the call of disturbed birds, anxious, loud-noised. But now grouse and snipe give way to black-headed gull, hoarse calling, perky walking. And to soaring herring gulls and the black and white society dress of the hard-working, long-beaked oyster-catchers. Now will shags and cormorants dive and sport and shake the water like the Saturday-afternoon girl at the pool. But this shaking and sporting and diving is done in the

business of living, and there is no stiffness of the shorthand week to be washed away.

Machynlleth with its parkland pastures and river with the rustling rushes and waving water flags. The Dovey, where Taliesin, the most famous of the Arthurian seers, was found. He was dis-

covered where the river runs into the sea, found by Elphin as he fished. Found as a baby, and the boy grew up with deep wisdom and eternal understanding of life and poetry.

Elphin was the young prince whose share of his father's fortune was to have been the Cantref-y-Gwaelod. But his portion was lost one night when a drunken overseer forgot to close the sluices. Only the dykes remain, St. Patrick's Causeway and out from Towyn the other, Sarn y Bwch. This latter almost joins with St. Patrick's Causeway and only the wise ones of Cardigan Bay can sail safe in the openings. Or dodge the white surf where the sea breaks over the old raised boundaries of the sunken land.

Up in the hills I can see the breaking line of water, the green of the sea turned savage foam as it slops over the walls of the talked-of land. And when the low tides of the year come, then the Causeway peeps into sight in places. But there can be no regaining now, for sea and sand and shell, the weight of water and the mysteries of the sea have come, and will remain.

An ache always in the marshes at the hinterland of the sea, where the dykes have been built, stone in stone, but the land has never been properly drained.

There is a great marsh to the one side of my house and a foot-path straight and lonely across the length of it. And with the great long graves lying in it, holes from where the peat has been dug out, filled now with quiet black water. Always water, in the drought of summer and in the rain of winter, never dry and never overflowing. The water never takes on the colour of the sky, or the length of reflected moonbeams. But always stagnant, despairing water. With a menace about it, the cotton plants grow straight by the side of it, afraid to bend over. Only in parts of the marsh is there the greenness. And that a colour of deceit, for one foot on the lovely lawn and the whole shivers and trembles. A horse and cart could slip in and leave only a scar on the green top. And in a few weeks all would be smooth and tempting again.

Marshland bog and peaty turf, a share of this land in North Wales. Where the streams run brown and the water has the flat, peaty taste. Rush in the wetter places and on the edge of the brooks great-headed marsh reeds rustle their stalks, fairy crinolines in the gentle wind. And when the wind is high and the great white clouds drift before a full moon then close your eyes on the bog. And then the noise in the reeds has all the anger of fast-walking women in it.

Up in the mountains the farmers dig peat from the upland bogs and peat moors. Cutting and stacking it out to dry in long, low walls. And when dry taking it on the horse-drawn sledge to the farmhouse. Storing the crumbling, brittle bricks in tidy piles against the house wall, covered with layers of old sacks. With perhaps a sheet of rusted corrugated iron on the top.

Peat which burns with the sweet smell of old earth and remembered, worn tweed. And gives a memory of great-eyed spaniels and the red fling of empty cartridge cases.

On the coast is Aberystwyth, holiday resort and remembered by the sunshine. A recommended place last century, with the bathing machines efficient and the attendants courteous. Aberystwyth with its Constitution Hill and the college by the sea. The curving bay and the prom. with its walking students, a kick to the bar at the one end for the sake of tradition.

Aberystwyth now the place for sunshine, ice cream, and the summer visitor. Here once were the lead mines which gave a hundred ounces of silver from every ton of lead. Mines which made Sir Hugh Myddleton a rich man, he who lost his fortune in the making of the New River to supply the north side of London with water.

Between the estuaries of the Dovey and the Mawddach the sea meets land smoothly. The headlands on the coast of Merionethshire dip slowly. With a rising slope from the sea and a greenness, and only just below the Mawddach near Llwyngwril does sudden cliff meet sea. The fields roll down from the mountains to the sea. Long, gentle, bright green slopes with the grey lines of the weathered stone walls. Little folds made sometimes in the corners of the fields for the sheep-gathering or shelter for the hardy black cattle, long-haired and long-horned; standing backs to the stone walls when the storm whines the rain straight from the sea. Tear and shriek and a hiss in the holes between the rounded stones. Rain beating against the hillside. Draining away to the sea again with trickle and long, silver waterfall in the gulleys of the rocks.

Here between the wideness of the estuaries the land curves down to the sea and all is neatly farmed. The houses built in some shoulder of the hill for protection. Some farms by the edge of the sea and built of the rounded, sea-smoothed stones. And with the front doors facing the mountains and only a great blank wall of house to the bleak, open sea. And in these days when men come to retire from the cities to the lonely beauty of the coast here, then they build with great sun parlours glinting Kew Gardens to the sea. A wonderful glass for the wind to hit and the rain to smear. Glass to break in the wild January storms, putty to be crumbled away by the heavy autumn rains. And the brine is left on the glass, salty, and making a private frostiness so that there is no seeing the last white horse when the last wind blows away.

Between the two estuaries are the towns of Aberdovey and Towyn, the villages of Fairbourne and Llwyngwril. Ungaudy places and they have kept away the golden paint and the gleaming sign. Kept their places very lovely and near to the great wide beaches and the mountains, with Cader Idris and mid-Wales a near journey.

This coast is quiet except in the summer, when the railway brings the visitors from the Midlands, and beyond. The coast railway which comes through little tunnels over the sea and an argument always between the engineer and Cardigan Bay. Pile and boulder and concrete and schemes eternal. Always the constant slap of the waters, the long, white-topped curl of the breakers. Breaking and sloshing and the white foam running quickly to the sea again. The sand ever changing and the patterns and the ridges fantastic, drying in the sunshine between the tides. And changed again with the next tide, smooth and sober, flat and planed level by the sea. Tempting to the man with the walking stick, the fancy golfing shoes leaving the pattern, and the deeper holes of the sinking stick. Or the bare Man Friday footsteps of a fisherman out to a net, cunning in a quiet cove. Or children with little sticks and white shells making ugly faces on the sand.

All to go to-night when the tide comes in. And to-morrow another ridge, another shape.

These the only invaders now. Who come by train and loving the place, for there are no lidos here, no car parks bigger than the beaches.

But there are memories here. Coming in with the wind at night, or at early morning when it has rained all night and the last drops make a rainbow before the sunshine, a horse-shoe from mountain to the sea. Memories of the Danes who landed here on the coast, easy to beach on the estuaries of the Mawddach and the Dovey. Easy on the shingle beaches and the soft sand. Landing, and then the plunder, the sad cry of women against the sea. The raiding Danes and the raiding Goidels coming to land on easy Merioneth-shire. And in the ordered days of the Romans the galleys up the Dovey, a deeper river and a landing-place for stores. And taking away all the ores and the gossip back to the south. The memory, too, of the Spanish galleon which came up the Dovey in the late sixteenth century. How it anchored there and landed its men, of the fighting, and how it sailed away again, the Welsh leaving it go.

On a moonlight night stand on the shores of the Dovey and look to the south, the dark hills of South Wales edging the sky. Look up-river and remember all the boats which have been. The Phœnicians and the smugglers. Spanish ship and neat Roman boat. And remember that around here King Arthur buried one of his Knights in Y Domen Las. Catch a whole armful of history.

Where now only the small boats, yacht and brassy, slip across from Ireland.

Towyn has its Bird Rock. A roost and noise eternal.

Llwyngwril with its little stream fighting boulders, the fresh, clear water twisting the last rocks to the sea. Rocks which have the gleaming marble streaks. And strands of seaweed wash up with the tide, brown and green and with the air bubbles cracking and breaking as the foot falls.

Stand on Llwyngwril shore, here where the Quakers once settled. A run from persecution and as far west as they could go. They have left a burial ground here, with the date over it.

The seagulls rest white and bobbing on the sea, side to side, up and down. Waiting until the tide goes out, and then the scavenging, the scouring. Fly in the air and come down in the water again, graceful and with a careful fold of the wings to keep them dry. The quick-moving eye ready for the throwing hand.

I stand on the shore in the evening, with the last lightness going fast and all the gulls coming in from the sea to sleep on the inland rocks. Flying quiet and fast for the sandman.

The road between Llwyngwril and Fairbourne rises high over the headland. A neat, well-made road with the concrete foundations, for ever the fear of the landslide to the sea.

Fairbourne with its great sickle of sand, its dreary windswept houses. Fresh in the summer and a beach for the swim, the snooze in the sun. In the winter the winds and the rain and the blowing sand, bleak and open to the sea.

Sanded Fairbourne is at the mouth of the estuary. The estuary of the Mawddach is wide and lovely. Across the mouth they have built a railway bridge, a great sound wooden bridge, three-quarters of a mile long. Made of the many cross-pieces so that there shall be no easy view out to sea. To distant Bardsey and soft blue Lleyn Peninsula. But a wonderful bridge to stand on and see far into Wales. And only the soot and the cinder and the tremble behind to say Paddington lies, a convenience, waiting.

I stand on the bridge, this would be an easy way, with a foot-bridge, a clanking turnstile and a waiting hand, to walk into Barmouth. But I shall take the way around, down the side of the estuary and through Dolgelley.

From this bridge I look deep into Wales, up this great estuary with the miles inland and the distant width. A lake when the tide is high. A golden desert of sand trickled with the ever-remaining river, when the tide is out. And above are the mountains, blue with stone, green and red and yellow with bracken and gorse and heather. Squares of green fields in the hollows of the hills, the smoke of distant hidden houses. A poster of a view, coloured, un-signed. The thousand acres black under the shadow of one cloud. The rest gay and light with sunshine. And the light and the black-ness moving and changing. Chasing old and new shadows moun-tain to mountain.

The tide runs fast from the wide waters of the estuary out through the narrow mouth to the sea at Barmouth. A surge and a noise to the moving of the tides, coming in, going out. The sand lifted and settled again in a new place. Fish up with the sea-water and the fishermen go out in bobbing boats up the estuary, hold fast with stout rope and small iron anchor. The lines baited with cut shellfish or wriggling sand worm, red yarn or mouldy cheese. The string of hooks, evilness hidden by the tasty morsel, the spike concealed. A twist of seaweed around the line, camouflage deceptive. The lead sinkers tied on carefully and the long throw far out to the water. A splash, the sit down, the cigarette rolled, the pipe bowl scraped, the wait.

Twitch at the line and the flat and the round fish hauled in, slipping and twisting. The hooks re-baited, the fish caught dancing silver, ever slower in the basket.

Slack water comes and after that the turn of the tide. The shud-der to the still water and after the race out to sea again, the great magnet drawing. The boats land again, the fish sold to shops and to the boarding-houses.

I look down at the green water, in swirl and twist and suck as it meets the stout wooden piles of the bridge. A dark depth with circling foam and cauldron seething as bottom currents surge to the top.

And under the edge of the low cliff, under the first houses of Barmouth, the little white boat is anchored against the rock.

Anchored in an odd, definite way so that the wood is held firm and secure against the rock. Way up on the cliffside a little iron anchor tucked into a crevice, into a slot among the black and the green of the seaweed at the dark water-line of the high tide. And from the rusted anchor a stout rope trails over the wet seaweed to the stern of the boat. Passing there through a ring and on again from the front of the boat to another anchor on the far side. So that the boat is held secure with only the up and the down of the currents to sway it with tap and pat against the rock.

In the rowing-boat is a fisherman. Not a rod-and-line man or the city businessman on doctor's orders for the fresh air. But a professional in oilskin trousers and a high-necked black sweater. With a peaked cap jaunty over one ear. And on the other ear the short, blackened white stump of a cigarette.

He is musselling. Raking in the shellfish clinging in their thousands to the river bottom. These to be raked up and sorted and packed and sent away by passenger train, a hasty, tasty meal for town and city.

He is using a long-handled rake. A fifteen-foot handle straight into the water by the side of the anchored boat. A pressing down with the full weight of his body, a scrape and a pause, feet wide apart in the boat. Then pull and the rake brought up hand over hand, carefully and steadily. The mussels dripping and grey, mixed up with broken-away rock and twisted seaweed. The whole tipped with a bang and a shake into a square wooden box. Then the arms send the rake down again with pull and lift for another full catch. At the end of the afternoon the fisherman goes back to the harbour and the shellfish are sorted in little outhouses on the quay. Packed into boxes and addressed and sent away on the evening mail train to the retailers. Fresh shellfish, tender from the sea for to-morrow's eating.

Higher up the estuary on the edge of the water-line are cockles for the lifting. But a colder job this, with a back-bending and turning over of the sand and the stray seaweed. And between the sand patches there are rocks to be climbed over. Rubber boots sink in the sludge and the wet sand sucks. A boot left behind and then a balancing on one foot, the basket laid carefully on some shelf of rock. The boot regained and then on again. Search in sand and a pause sometimes to straighten the back and look at the shape of the sky, feel the edge of the wind.

Some of the seagulls have a cunning way with the hard shellfish. After a storm the sand is blown loose at every tide and the gulls are busy in the estuary. The sand is driven in great moving screens and in between the gusts the gulls settle and pick up exposed shells. But no pausing to peck and struggle. But fly high over the causeways and the rocks. Fly high and drop the shells straight on the hardness. A crunch and the shell splays open. With flapping wings and curving head the bird drops straight.

The view inland is Merionethshire, the mountains seen wild and many shaped from the estuary bridge. And a place to get lost in, Merionethshire. The farms with the high mountain acres and the sheep brought down in the thousand. The time of shearing and of dipping. Shepherds going up the high little valleys in between

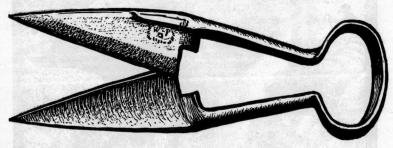

the mountains. Where the little streams run and the water is brown with peat. Rush and green bog by the road up into the hills, the easy way. Following the stream to bring the sheep down. Man on horse or on the bicycle. Old black suit, once first Sunday best, kept for the preaching meetings and the funerals. Then second Sunday best for the everyweek Sunday. And when, with the years, the fringe has come to the trousers' bottom, then used for the best everyday special occasion, market and sheep sales. And now, at last, the everyday suit. The black turned green on the shoulders and the sudden shine on the knees in the sunshine.

Bringing the sheep down from the hills with dog and bike. A wonderful bicycle, too, kept oiled and clean and everlasting new. Green enamelled with the chain whirring smooth in an oil-bath case. The brakes working deep inside the handlebars. And a step at the back to get on. And over the peak of the back mudguard the carrier, with the greased brown straps folded neatly.

Mountain roads with the shale loose at the sides and the rounded stone of the foundation smoothing through at the sides. Big stones taken from the streams and used as the base of the road. By the sea, too, there are the rounded stones in the walls and the cottages.

Up into the mountains. The stone walls straight and steep and made once in the sweating hours. No mortar, but a snug crevicing of each stone into the awkward shape of the next. Straight up a mountain, lasting all the drifts of blizzard, the sudden rolls of blue

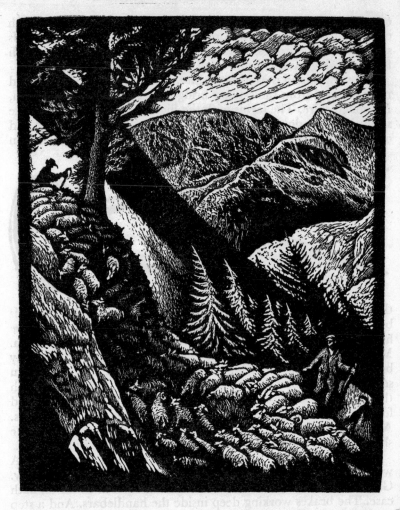

boulder. In the making each stone an individual. Each corner and
each up-and-down turned in the hand to fit. Walls straight up
into the blue, past the blaze of gorse and the crimson smear of
heather, faint rustling and the sudden gleaming white of sheep
bones left bare.

The sheep are rounded down from the mountains by the dogs.
Three or four working to the distant signal of the faint sharp
whistle. Small Welsh mountain sheep tumbling and jumping down
to the valley for the shearing or the dipping.

The farms of the hills with the small house and the speck of outbuilding. No barned home farm or with the straight, tidy cow-houses smelling sweet with disinfectant. Only the two or three cows kept for the milk and the butter. Churned once a week. The milk "separated" each night, a turning of handles and the whirr of cogs. Two spouts and from the one thick, clogging cream. From the other the separated milk used to feed the calves, to fatten the pigs. The cream set aside and left to thicken on the black hob of the kitchen fire. And on the day of churning taken and poured into the great rounded barrel of the churn. The drops of butter colour poured gently in. And then the hours of the turning. A handle oiled and working smooth out from the churn. End over end for the morning. The observation glass at the top come clear, the screws are opened. The buttermilk poured away for hens or pigs. The small rounded lumps of butter all pressed together and are made, the salt added, and the fancy patterns set with the wooden tools.

The shearing often done now with the machines. A handle turned or a motor started. Gone the week of clip-clip. The bright hand-shears smeared now with vaseline and used only in the summer maggot trimming to take away the little wool. Soon the bright hand-shears will twinkle with the firelight, hooked to hearthside with the cheese samplers and the gay horse brasses. Become the ornament and once every week made white with polish, to gleam again for the evenings. Peat square in the open chimney. A peep up and half-way there the iron bar across. And clanging black from it the long chain with the hook to hang the kettle.

The sheep sheared and the wool made into the neat bundles. Packed tight into the canvas bags, ready to be taken down into town and the wait for the dealers. Men who have lived once in distant Bradford. And who come with the brown overalls and one sleeve rolled up. A deep feel far into the heart of the wool. A pinching there of the fleece and the bringing out of a tiny sample. Nipped tight between thumb and finger-nail. Held to the light and pulled slowly apart. The offer made, accepted.

On both sides of the Mawddach estuary there are the roads. Twisting and snaking round rock and searching always for the flat land near the water. When the tide is high there is the twinkle through the trees and the vision of salt blueness, stretching away in small waves to the distant, other wooded side. The two roads reach Dolgelley, town in shadow of the mountains and small and low, for what chimney or high slate roof can compete with Cader Idris?

A town of streets criss-cross with sharp turnings. A sad town, Dolgelley, with its sober stone and anxious always at the foot of the giants. Cader, god of the mountain, he who made the first harp and was a great bard and studied the stars from his seat in the sky. Up there, blue and black, his mountain home with the mists and the record of the souls chased and caught. The dead who, in after-life, try to live in the crevices and gulleys of his mountain, and Cader, a hunter as well as a bard, claims them for his own.

Coming into Dolgelley I feel always a smallness and a Humpty-Dumpty fear that the mountains will come suddenly down, the three thousand feet levelled smooth.

Dolgelley is the county town of Merionethshire. With Cader Idris to give it fame and the visitors coming off the trains with hob-nailed boots. Corseted in coils of rope and looking up defiantly to the mountains. The train steaming away and the last air of the city lost for the fortnight. The battle is on every summer. Cader and his friends of the mountains standing still and waiting for the slip of boot, the fray of rope, the sudden break of nerve.

A cowed town, Dolgelley, as if waiting for the great whip which never falls.

And here is Cader Idris, great mountain with the mystic chair. Up three thousand feet and the first of a long range of mountains to the Arenigs and the Arans. The view from the top to Cardigan Bay and east across Wales to the Border and beyond.

The old tales linger. He who stays the night on Cader Idris (the Chair of Idris) and sits the dark hours in the Chair, he will become a madman, a corpse, or a poet.

Around Cader are the lakes, Llyn y Gader and Gwernam, and the waterfalls.

Idris, a giant of the mountains, and a hunter. Persistent with his dogs hunting the souls of the departed who may have taken refuge in the blue crevices and misty heights of his mountain, a rival to Satan and his Hounds of Hell who hunt the county of the Berwyn Mountains.

Cader Idris can now be climbed without the guides. Those who once conducted parties to the top of the mountain. In the *Post Chaise Companion through Wales* we read of Robert Edwards, who, at the end of the eighteenth century, "by all Divine assistance conducted to, and over, the most tremendous mountain, Cader Idris, to the stupendous cataracts of the Cayne and the Mawddach, and to all the enchanting cascades of Dol-y-Melynllyn. Guide general and magnificent expounder of all the natural and artificial curiosities of Nortn Wales, professor of grand and bom-

bastic lexicographical words, knight of the most anomalous whimsical (yet perhaps happy) order of hair-brained inexplicables". He was dressed in a blue coat, with yellow buttons, a pair of old boots and a cocked hat with a feather of tremendous size. The way is lonelier now to the top of Cader, with flowing word and phrase gone. And only the grunts and city jokes of the hikers and the summer-dressed ones to speak the way.

Out from the town a lonely road goes to Bala. And to Llangadfan a lonelier road. This rising steeply out of Dolgelley town, thankful to reach up out of this grey child of Cader Idris. Rises steep up and then the long journey over the moors and through the pass of Dinas Mawddwy. Farms far and few, long miles in the hills, whitewashed and clear, and with the sheep paths reaching out from them, brown and narrow. The mountains green with bracken in the summer, becoming brown in the autumn. Sometimes the bracken cut with the scythe and come in to the farms on sledges. Flat, foot-high tables with iron runners underneath. Pulled by a single horse and able to go easily up and down the mountains, the runners humming over the scorched bare grass. Able to go where an ordinary farm cart would topple because of its height and the steepness of the slope. This sledge piled high with the dried fern and the load goes bouncing away along the hillside to the loft built over the cowhouse. There, or in some out-building, the bracken is stored for the winter. And when the hard weather comes it will be taken down, a precious pitchforkful at a time, and used as litter for the cattle, to make a soft clean warm bed to lie on. And when this fresh litter has become soiled it is not carried out straightway, but fresh fern is laid straight on the top. Then when spring comes the solid, caked bedding is cut with a big two-handed hay knife. Sliced up and carried outside and put as manure on the fields which will be kept for the summer hay. The manure will be carried out in a farm cart and pulled down from the back of it with a long L-shaped two-pronged fork into little heaps on the fields. In leisurely time garden forks are taken out to the fields and the manure is spread evenly over the grass from the black-yellow heaps. Spread over the field and after that the cattle are kept out and the grass grows for the summer hay. These few good fields on a mountain farm which keeps only a few cattle, and sheep must be the main living.

The fields to be kept for hay are gate-fastened and the cattle kept away and the grass grows green and long and tender. In the valleys the hay harvest starts in May, but on the hill farms it is much later. And in most of the valley and the hill farms there is as yet little mechanisation of the hay harvest. There is much communal effort among the smaller farmers. Hay-cutting machines, swathe turners and tedders for the hay shaking, all are expensive for the small farmer to use only for a few days in the twelvemonth. And horse rakes take space to store, so that there is much lending and much borrowing. Much helping of one farm with the labour from the next.

Some of the big farms in the Vales of Clwyd, Llangollen and Conway and in mid-Wales are using silage, storing the grass wet and green with the addition of molasses. And some of these modern farms are using elevators and balers and newfangled devices. But for the small North Wales farmer the harvest is much the same now as it has been for the many years. The difference is that now there are the mowing machines where in the old days there were the scythe teams. And now there are wide horse rakes where once the hay was raked rustling into rows with two-handed rakes.

The hay is cut early in the morning so that the heat of the day will not tire the horses. And the night before there has been a sniff at the wind, a tap at the barometer, a half-listening to the weather forecast, and only if fine weather seems certain is the hay cut. For rain means trouble and more manipulation before the hay is ready to carry.

The mowing machine leaves the hay in neat swathes. Then on the second or third day, if the sun has been good, the rows are turned over with a horse-pulled swathe turner with revolving, lifting prongs. Or sometimes turned by hand with rake and pitchfork. And after that the hay is shaken and raked into long rows across the field. Comes the cocking, piling the hay into small heaps in the Border country. But in the mountains these heaps are small stacks on the field. The small cocks are carried into barn or made into one great stack after a few days. But the larger piles are left sometimes for several weeks before the final carrying.

Haymaking, and the memory to me of brown explosive homemade ginger beer, smashing out the cork and covering the hands with foam and froth. A memory, too, of summer afternoons in some small dark hayloft with the sun dancing heat on the blue slates above. A memory of tea in the open cool of the shade of some stack or hedge. Each with a little thistle-free cushion of hay to sit on. An ache in the knees and the good pain of straightening tired shoulders. Tea in the open and the buzz of black flies around the jam-pot and the waving away. Bess, the horse, rattling her bucket of water, flapping her big lips on the handle and enjoying the smell of the water before she drinks. Half-way through she gives a great flabbering of lips and a long shake in the jingling harness. Tea over and then back to the pitching of the cocks of hay high to the top of the load. Up there is the loader with a short-handled pitchfork, setting the hay to a safe square load. And holding tight at every warning shout as the horse is moved on between the rows.

The field is cleared and only the last rakings to be got in to-morrow, and to-night's last load will be unloaded in the morning. A three-legged support is set under the hay wagon and Bess is unloaded. A slap on her back and she trots away. The back of the harvest is broken and we are ready for autumn rain and winter snow and the cold wind of March. The summer has been gathered in and the sunshine laid safely away.

A healthy road this, from Dolgelley to Dinas Mawddwy and beyond to Llangadfan. A great, steep pass, sign-posted red, and with the warnings stark on the boards: *Dangerous Hill. Heavy Vehicles Change Down.* Short white posts hold up these warnings, writings for those who do not know the Bwlch Oerddrws Pass. A run down the green-banked road, steep into the pit. A peering over the rim and the road runs right over with a turn, another sign. The breath caught again with the sweep of the mountains, the distance of the tiny farms. A look back, the head steeped to the height. Watching the road going up to the sky, the horizon the end of the way. Stand and watch a car coming over, blue fly on the edge of the table.

At the bottom of the main hill the road gentles down into the village of Dinas Mawddwy. An Alpine place with the feel of the mountains, the sway of conifers, larch and fir and pines by the roadside, and a healthy greenness everywhere. A clean, good place, Dinas, with trim, home-cut poles carrying the electricity made by a mountain stream. Borrow called this a "dirty, squalid place". But clean and sweet now and a place to rest the spirit in, to make the body pulse again.

For centuries the road from Dolgelley through Dinas has been a great highway out of the North-West of Wales into England. A road for packmen and for merchants and for the official travellers. But not always a safe way, this gaunt pass tempting in its loneliness outlawed soldiers and wanted felons. In the sixteenth century here were the Gwylliaid Cochion Mawddwy' (the Red-haired Bandits of Mawddwy). And Queen Mary gave a commission to a Baron Lewis to settle this roguery. He and his men captured eighty of the bandits and they were hanged on Christmas Eve. A watching mother bared her breasts and said that other sons had sucked there and that they would dip their hands in the blood of the Baron. And so it happened that he was on his way home from the Assizes on All Hallows E'en and he was killed. And it is said that the brothers dipped their hands in the murdered man's blood, so sweet was the revenge. But all ordered now and policeman's blue.

Two miles away from Dinas is Mallwyd, where once John Davies was the vicar. A believer in simple rites for the Church and compiler of a Welsh-Latin dictionary. Working here in the mountains, and news from England and beyond no faster than a man's journey. Worries of a neighbour the worry of the parish.

Out from the mountain village of Dinas Mawddwy a road to Bala. Under the heights of the two Arans, Aran Mawddwy with its thirty feet off three thousand and Aran Benllyn. Under their majesty and through this pass with the wonderful name of Bwlch-y-Groes—The Pass of the Cross. This high pass where old tales tell that there was once a cross, gaunt and in shadow against the sky. So that travellers lifting their eyes to the weary road might see the symbol of hope.

Back to Dolgelley, for I must go to the edge of the sea again. Trying to catch the spirit of a village, the bare sense of glory on a windy heather hill, the security and lush plenty of a well-watered valley. Things taken for granted except at the stray odd times. A slant of sunshine yellow through summer thunder clouds and a roving spotlight on the faint miles of crimson heather. Or the water meadows in the valley when the cowman leans over a gate and calls with a slow "Bo-Hoop" to the black-and-white and white-and-red cattle, time to come in for the milking. The moment when the load of corn comes from some far field through the village street. The raw ends of sheaves sticking out and stray corn falling out from the bottom of the wagon, and the red hens come trotting out from behind the blacksmith's shop for the quick, worried pecks. And the only excitement when a new tractor is bought. Or a threshing machine or one of the last cider mills passes through.

Once the cider mills went on creaking wooden wheels from farm to farm. A high, wooden box with the rollers inside to grind and pulp the cider apples. And a chute, a narrow, wooden trough banded with delicate, wrought iron-work to take away the juice. The mill driven by a portable steam boiler or by a horse. The animal walking round at the end of a long pole centred to a sort of windlass with greased cogs and geared to move eventually fast. Some of the farms have these horse-powered systems to pulp root crops and to work the chaff-cutters, the latter in which straw is cut by a quick-revolving knife into tasty pieces for the cattle food. But now most of the farms work their machines from diesel engines or petrol motors, often at the same time making electricity as a by-product for farm and house lighting.

The cider mills do not travel now. The one which I used to see once or twice in the year is now rusting away in the untidy yard of the local scrap-iron merchant. The outside red boards have been stripped away and the bare inside cogs and rollers and sieves are open to the weather. The wooden wheels are breaking apart and sinking slowly in the earth and the whole is waiting with the stacked horse-shoes and the old broken farm implements, waiting for the day when the price of scrap will reach the peak price. Then it will be loaded away to the scrap foundry and the last of the cider mills will have gone. The last of the cider makers has gone already, he a lame little man who walked with the horse who pulled the mill. His bicycle slung on the top of the machine, the wheels twisted and spinning with the jolts of the road. The mill delivered to the farm, the little man would ride away home for the night, his one leg hanging straight by the side of his bicycle. And his other cord-trousered leg working quickly the one pedal of the fixed-wheel bike.

Every farm made the cider and this was the harvest drink. And the quality of the cider was often an enticement to the harvest workers, for the cider was free and in plenty. There was an art in the making, and some of the farm wives used to drop in the fresh meat into each cask, as a something for the cider to "work on".

Now the harvest drinks are the bought bottled beers on the non-chapel farms. And on the T.T. farms it is the shop squash or the non-alcoholic home-brewed beer.

And buttermilk. That still is a favourite drink, cool and satisfying with the thought of meadow buttercups and cow-eaten, fragrant grasses.

Buttermilk, too, is used to make the girdle cakes of flour and salt, and baked on a hot iron laid direct on the coals of the fire. The cakes are split into two and buttered hot. Delightful with a faint toughness to the outside iron-baked crust.

Tea, of course, strong Welsh tea which seems on the brew all day. A cup for the postman and for the men at the "little lunch" often in the morning. This either eaten in the field at the manure-spreading or at the hedge-cutting. But if near the house, then in there for the tea and the cheese and the bread.

I travel out from Dolgelley, on the way to Barmouth. My way will be on the lovely road which runs the estuary side and under the mountains, to end with the sea.

On this twisted, wooded road through Llanelltyd is Cymmer Abbey. A Cistercian House with lancet windows and ruins like an old, worn, broken tooth. The Cistercians were sheep farmers and interested always in a good pastoral site, with meadows fair and unfailing water. Siting their abbeys by water meadows and backed by the hills on which to graze the sheep. A ruin now and the sheep farming done by the Welsh chapel folk, with Mass and rosary and chant things hated as coming from Satan himself. And the only memory of the old religion in the way the Welsh girl wets her finger and makes a quick cross on her breast for a sign that she speaks the utter truth. Roman Catholicism is a thing hated by the chapels. The only Catholic churches are in some of the seaside and in some of the market towns. The countryfolk are all staunch Protestant, with Nonconformity in the majority. The Church in Wales does not dare to put on too much haberdashery, too much colour or glory. And I have heard the Nonconformist ministers praying for the souls of those who are in the grip of Satan's Catholic friends.

There is gold in the Merioneth hills. And once mined in the many places around Dolgelley. But now the Welsh gold comes from near Bontddu only. There in the mountains between Barmouth and Dolgelley. Quarrying and crushing and a search for the yellow metal. Used for Royal wedding rings and the ornaments of princes.

The great Gold Fever came to Merionethshire in 1862. A rush and an excitement, an opening of mines and hope high for the golden dust. Mines named the Prince of Wales and the St. David, the Sovereign and the East Cambrian, the Vigra and Clogau. But now the mines are closed and the excitement has gone. With only the Bontddu mine to supply the Welsh gold when Royal occasion demands.

But the sand of the Mawddach estuary, too, has a preciousness. For the experts say that here all the gold dust of the centuries has been washed down. Brought by the rivers from the mountains, an erosion of the gold foundations. The dredgers have not yet come and only the oyster-catchers dig in the sand. And no farm labourer comes down by the shore with washing pan and an eye for the edge of gold. No long search for the precious dust in the leisure hours.

How do the people spend their leisure time? The hours after work on the lonely farms, the winter evenings when darkness comes early and the milking has to be done with the light of the storm lanterns, or the stable lamps as they are called.

Paraffin is the important thing of the winter. A drum of it, forty or twenty gallons, on bricks in an outhouse. A brass, long-handled tap at the bottom and a spout and funnel. The lamps filled from the drum. Some of the farms use the yellow light from two-burner paraffin lamps for light in the house in the evenings. An iron stand with a brass or glass reservoir on the top. The glass a ruby red or a dull soft green, with the long wick dipping in, snake curled over. A glass chimney, cleaned twice a week with the crumpled-up local paper twisted inside. And around the glass chimney a fancy globe of frosted glass. So that the gentle light comes only with a dim glow, and spectacles at thirty for those who read at night.

The electric grid reaches only the more populated towns and the villages on the lines in between. Some of the villages make their own private supply from turbines or water-wheels. Often the old flour mill is used and the dynamo whirrs where once the big grinding stones slipped smoothly. The cells of batteries straight and orderly where once the flour bags were piled high, or the wheat waited in the still bags for the chute. But most of the old flour mills are quiet now, the water running through the broken wheel and crows flying through the open rafters. And only the deep mill ponds used for fishing, the spinning for pike with whirr of reel and the hope for the sudden pull at the running line.

Some of the farms have their own electric-lighting systems. And the two-burner lamps are now being replaced by the paraffin incandescent lamps with the gas-like mantles.

Paraffin is used for cooking on many farms. But most of the houses still use the old heavy kitchen ranges, black and with the many flues. The oven on the one side and on the other the small boiler with a brass tap sticking out over the tin fender. A lift-up lid to the boiler and a jug of cold water poured in every time a jug of hot is taken away from the tap. Hot water for the washing-up, or the hot-meal feed for the calves. These ranges take much coal and logs. The coal stored often in the yard outside, the black heap of it seen miles away, stark, against the colours of the mountain-side. The logs are from a tree felled with an axe, then sawn up into short lengths and carried to the farm. Perhaps split into pieces with iron wedges and a swinging wooden mallet. Or put on the wooden horse and the whirr-whirr and the clean, fresh sawdust from a cross-cut saw. The logs dropping off and stacked neatly; a mosaic for the winter; in barn or empty stable.

The spare time, then? In the winter nights and the still, gnat-infested summer evenings? When the rain comes and water pours all day into the tubs under the drain-pipes. Soft water, sacred and precious for washing-day, blue and the sweet smell of hot wet clothes. Summer nights when the swallows pitch low, fly high. And in the cities they talk of cricket and the pub doors are fastened wide back, the stained-glass windows slid right down. When the landlord rolls up his sleeves and the sweat of his hands slips the white handles.

Evenings when the work is done, and what of the half-day? Sunday, when all cannot go to chapel three times.

The family of the farm live in the front kitchen. The servant men and the girl live in the back kitchen. And by the fire in either kitchen a lot of the winter evening time is passed away.

When young, there is the courting. When old, the preparation for Sunday. Those who have no character in the parish go to the pub. Those who prepare for Sunday, they do not go to the pub. For Welsh Nonconformity fights always the "drink menace". A lot of their prayers go towards it, a lot of their preaching.

In the Welsh countryside there is very little playing of games. Seldom is heard in Welsh village the crack of bat and ball. Seldom the sweet excitement of cricket. Never the blacksmith who hits beyond the far green tree. The village schoolmaster who umpires with the stern, unblinking eye.

Football is popular in mid-Wales. Saturday afternoon and the games in the various leagues. With a collection and a line of people on the touch-line. All week the pitch has been pasture with sheep grazing. But on Saturday the stock are turned away with waving stick and barking dog to the next field. Midday the secretary of the local football comes with tape and sawdust and small boys. And the village carpenter brings the goal-posts, white and fresh, taken up after each match. The goal-posts long and bright, and indecent brought on the bier which other days is used for the funerals. The posts raised and slid into flush sockets on the meadow. The lines of sawdust made and measured and all is ready for the match. The away team come, change in their motor coach. Walk onto the field, white knees showing and legs awkward with the shin pads.

The village and small town pubs have the darts and the Darts League matches. The winter tournaments, and the silver cup, gleaming in its glass case, will twinkle away the summer sunlight in the winning pub parlour.

Courting is a sport, an organised pastime, especially in the mountains. The ride on bicycle for the lonely miles and the hope high in the heart that she will be there. That there will be no thorns or tacks on the road and no sudden hiss of air, harsh grate of road on rim of metal wheel.

An affair of gates and mossy ditches and snug haystacks, Welsh mountain courting. With a wonderful gala night at times of concerts and Eisteddfodau.

Eisteddfodau and concerts. Things not to be missed.

And in some of the hill farms they have singing to the harp, the penillion singing peculiar to Wales. Two or three harpists and singers gathering together in the stone-flagged kitchen. Sweet plucking of the harp and the passionate singing. Far into the night with cups of tea and home-made scones.

People of the North and the South enjoy singing, and hymns sung in chapels always have the melody. Bass and tenor and alto and soprano. The new member to the chapel always noted for his register and the tone of his voice.

Chapels, condemned and praised, sweet and ugly. Narrow-minded and big-hearted. Deacons who hate cinemas and dances and the drama and all things of the flesh. Yet in their singing a joy and at all times a wonderful neighbourliness one to another. And when trouble comes, no need to lift a finger. For they all will be there.

Early travellers tell of the pigs which slept in Barmouth streets. Now where children clank spade against gay bucket and the ladies walk peach and pink in bathing costume.

Barmouth, grey-stoned and little-harboured, is at the mouth of the Mawddach estuary. A sea wall on the one side and the rising height of the cliff at the back. In between, the town. Tight against the smooth concrete and at the back the streets pushed up and built on ledges on the cliffs. Reached by winding stepped paths and roads and with the view over the dark chimney-pots and back doors and out to sea. Old Barmouth this clinging part of the town. With old stone cottages and fairyland sugar-loaf houses with bright brass knockers and flower-potted windows.

The town has a long main street and side streets with a peep of the sand, the first white petticoat waves of the sea. In the summer the men with walking-sticks and the young girls with ready cameras. And on a Saturday the great changing over. The week's visitors going off with the morning train, money paid, and with the neat greaseproof packets of sandwiches. In the afternoon the next week's visitors coming and the boarding-houses and the private hotels do the shuffling over of sheets and pillow-cases and a hasty rinse of tablecloths in the basement kitchens. Judgments made and character fortified for the stay. Kiddies itching for the beach, clinking the pavements with spade and painted bucket. Every good bedroom in the summer is given over to the visitors. During the season the landlady and her shopping husband sleep in bare iron-bedded attics. Or when the house is quiet and *they* have all gone to bed comes the setting up of a trestle-bed in the kitchen. And always the alarm clock set early. Enough has to be made in the season for the empty winter months when the last crowded train has gone and only the sea builds castles in the sand.

There is a little black-watered harbour, snug at the mouth of the river, and a rounded, grey-stoned wharf. In the summer the harbour is coloured with the yachts and the painted boats. Yellow and red sails and even the phut-phut of the motor boats is lost when the wind blows over Ynys-y-Brawd fresh from the sea.

This island, Ynys-y-Brawd, the Isle of the Brother, green marram grassed, and with the sandy shore around it. Here, where once the Holy Hermit lived and Barmouth town was unknown, unbuilt. For the town is not ancient and once the mouth of the estuary was much wider and edged out to sea far below where balmy Barmouth now stands. Sand and silt came and the navigation demanded a new village. And the houses came where the boats anchored, and the new town grew.

Barmouth, where Taylor the Water Poet came on his Welsh Tour in 1652. And where he had *a hen boiled with bacon, as yellow as the cowslip, or gold noble.*

I live now across the estuary from Barmouth and my present journey is on the land I see each day. This seaside town where I go for all my weekly shopping. Where I buy paraffin and new wicks for the oil lamps. And where the sun always seems to shine in the winter and the only wind is from the west. Mild and warm and the cliff at the back of the town taking away all the cold winds from the north and the east. This town with its bright new sea wall and its lovely old unequal houses. Homes built of the squared grey stone and with fantastic chimney-pots to dodge the draughts and give the fires always a draw.

I walk home across the mouth of the estuary, walking the convenient bridge. On the one side the boom of the sea. And on the other the Ardudwy and the distant Aran mountains across the water of the wide estuary, and Cader Idris reflected blue.

This wonderful estuary, changing its moods and its colours; pliable to every wind, every change of sky.

68

And from my windows I can see the mountains and the magic of Diphwys. I lean back in my chair now and there it is across the water. Too high in its perfect shape to fit into my curtained window. Bend the head to see the top, capped now with December snow and whiter than the clouds which blow in gaily from the sea. To-morrow perhaps it will be rain and Diphwys will have his cap, a discreet model done in mist. But when the fine weather comes the snow will be gone and the old greenness I love so well will be back again. The mountain cone against the sail of clouds, or the bright of the stars when the hunter moon is high.

He has a heart of gold, so story tells. And in his bottom mountains they tunnel for gold now. But they'll never reach his heart. For he's an old giant with the stone walls along him and the sheep grazing his shoulders. And if his gentle heart is made of gold, then he'll have some sure way of waking before the last golden treasure is reached.

From Barmouth I go along the coast road to Harlech, salt-aired, stone-walled. Past Llanaber Church, perfect Early English and on the side above the sea. The graveyard sloping and only the black line of the railway between the dead and the sea. The gulls fly over, white and calling. High, and gliding back on the wind, sea to shore. Bending yellow beaks to the railway and the hope of the thrown bread with the half-circle of the unhappy bite.

Llanaber Church, quiet above the sea where the genius built it. This lovely, tiny church with the arch, and the sandstone pillars and the mellow, tinted glass, colours sacred. The road with the coast cars on the one side, and below the railway. This church once safe between the mountains and sea, secure between the equal giants. And the road was only a track and speed only the gallop of a horse. Where the railway now snakes, bright rails in the moonlight, was once sand and shore, the last of the land and the first of the sea.

Here was a door which once had the skin of a Danish pirate nailed to it. He who had been caught; flayed alive.

Off the road is the long approach drive to Cors y Gedol, Elizabethan house of the Vaughans, friends of Ben Jonson.

To Harlech, high Harlech, up on the heights above the curving bay. The town with its famous castle and its Men Marching. With a fine College for Adult Education and its golf links on Morfa Harlech.

This town on a hill before the sea with the view of misty blue Caernarvonshire and Tremadoc Bay. On the edge of a high cliff is the castle. Four-tower cornered, reeking with history and

memories of blood. Built by Edward the First on the site of an earlier tower where once had lived Bronwen, sweet Welsh-named daughter of Bran, a Christian chief. Her tower gone and the great stone castle built on this height of rock, where once was the drop to the sea. But the waters are giving back land here. Robbing a Peter on some crumbling coast to pay Paul here with the dunes, the drifting sand.

Visitors walk around the castle, jumping a little at the stone echoes. Flicking ash over the breathless drop from the walls; a craning neck, the holiday joke. This castle where queens have come, and Glyndwr, King of Wales.

West across the bay is the Lleyn peninsula of Caernarvonshire. But I shall go there later, from the north. Now it will be the heart of Wales again, back to the east. This is an uneasy land by the sea, the urge is now for valley and pasture again. Inland where sea is the one thing of the year for the summer holidays. Time full of sand and sail and fun. With never a thought for the driftwood white and well-burning which comes in after a storm. Never to see the bright-green hollow balls of glass washed up, floats from the nets which have broken away in the sudden wind.

The urge to stay here now only a little time, here by Tremadoc Bay. And then face to the mountains and the way through the valleys again.

Here on the shores of this bay once lived Shelley and once Lawrence of Arabia. The flat land of Traeth Mawr was stolen from the sea. A Mr. William Alexander Madocks, M.P., spent £100,000 and gained seven thousand sandy acres from the sea by embankment building. Once the tides came in salty, and full of their own particular life, where now the land is tilled. The M.P. from Boston in Lincolnshire with an urge to see flat, straight land as of his own constituency. Or perhaps the urge of the fen-man to fight the sea.

And helping him in this business was Shelley. He was living with his wife Harriet and her sister at Tan-yr-allt, a house built by Madocks. Shelley who was to drown in the Gulf of Spezia, far foreign waters from Welsh Tremadoc Bay.

The embankment remains, a mile long and with a hundred yards base. Like a mythical seaside sweetmeat, the stick of rock a mile long and goodness knows how thick, with the name all the way through it. This embankment secure against the sea and perhaps with a memory of strange, unhappy Shelley. He who spent four months only on this distant edge of Wales.

Tan-yr-allt is by Tremadoc, this place with its legend of Madog who sailed to the Americas, in his small ship, to find the New World. Sailing there and back again and his discovery recorded

only in talk and the gossip of the years. And all the credit going to Columbus, venturer where the Welsh sailor had already been.

Madog went to America, sailed back to Wales and took some of his countrymen on a second journey. The Welsh are supposed to have settled in Mexico or on the coast of Carolina. For those who have researched in the matter say that there are Welsh words in use among the Mexican Indians. And when the later settlers moved in there was a tribe of Welsh Indians to the west of the Mississippi.

I turn now to the east, and my way will be inland again. A face up the vale of Festiniog and a heart high for the mountains beyond.

Many of the North Wales mountains now have the greenness of the forestry plantations. The conifers planted in straight, spaced rows, with every now and again a wide drive left. This lane for an approach to the trees, a way in when the charts are taken down in some far-away office and the time has come for the felling.

The firs and the larches are carefully grown in the nurseries. Then transplanted out on the mountains, small, perfect-shaped Christmas trees, set in tidy lines down the mountainside. The plantations are wired off and great notices warning against forest fires are set up along the edges.

The trees are left to the quietness of the years. Green always and finding an affection in the scheme of the countryside. In summer with the dark shade under them and the dropped brown of the cones. And in winter the whole forest moving like a giant cornfield in the wind. The snow lingering on the close branches and the whole a fairyland of green and white up to the edge of the sky at the top of the mountain. A mysterious place always, the heart of a plantation, with only twilight there and the sky open only where a tree has failed and the bare, stunted branches snap to the hand with all pliable liveness gone. Only this view above, a manhole to the sky.

The plantations make green many of the mountain slopes and only after years comes the felling. The whine of saws and the crash of falling trees. A last sway of the branches and then all is still. Comes the trimming with clop of axe and the trunk is sawn into the ordered lengths for the pit-props. Brown, sawn-ended, and pillars made for some black cathedral, low-roofed, long-naved.

The wood is taken away through the valley villages, stacked straight in lorries. Or filled straight as soldiers in bleak railway trucks. The mountain summer winds and the defiant winter greenness packed into the narrow trucks and taken away. Ordered for the deep descent, for they say that beauty is made to use and blackness is more important than greenness, and a deep hole more precious than any steep mountain.

I go up the valley to Festiniog, the lovely valley watered by the Dwyryd, this river with the sweet name. Later losing its music to the name of Traeth Bach before the sea comes and Tremadoc Bay.

Up to the two towns, Festiniog and its partner, Blaenau Festiniog, the slate towns. Blue, quarried from the mountains in big slices. And then split with mallet and skill into the delicate sheets. Welsh slate famous through the centuries, enduring wind and rain and the blaze of sunshine. Untouched by bitter hail and the rime of frost. The mountain heart of Wales taken away for distant church and Flanders roofs. A new blue sky, a safe and certain roof. And almost everlasting, come wind and weather.

The wild east and north country around Festiniog has a desolate, lost feeling. Frightened, and with a great emptiness about the mountains, a sadness about the moors.

And I leave these grey towns with the lonely outsides and travel through Trawsfynydd down to the cowed Dolgelley town once again.

But on my way I turn to see the old road of Helen's Causeway. What a name for a road, Helen's Causeway. Not an A or a B but making the way a live, remembered thing. This Roman road from Wroxeter by Shrewsbury through mid-Wales to Caersws, on to Trawsfynydd beyond Dolgelley, and over the mountains to the Dee Valley. Helen's Causeway named after the daughter of a British prince and wife of the Roman Emperor Maximus.

On this wild road, where it passes from Trawsfynydd over the wild land between Festiniog and Bala, are the famous Graves of the Men of Ardudwy. Strange stones and barrows with much argument as to their origin. And only the slate mountains of Festiniog can perhaps tell the story, or the two Arenig Mountains. A time of history known only by the unspeaking heights of grass and rock. Or perhaps the secret lies in the lake near here of Llyn-y-Morwynion (The Lake of the Young Women), blue with its Alpine waters. Legend has it that once the men of the Clwyd Valley came to fight the men of Ardudwy. And the invaders from that lovely valley killed all the men of the Ardudwy vale. But the women refused to be taken and drowned themselves in this lake. And perhaps the graves are the graves of their menfolk, or perhaps the remains go back to a dimmer, stranger age. Now the fishermen angle the holiday away, with city desk and strict black monster telephone forgotten. Or the stray hikers come with map and compass. With shorts rubbing raw on sunburned knees and the walking sticks held in a clumsy way, a twirling nuisance.

Helen and her high causeway. This grand, once great, road with a width to it, and a view. Grassy now and the paved way covered with grassy soil. The fishermen and the hikers in the summer, the sheep and the foxes in the winter, walk along its lonely places, the long reaches of Helen's Causeway.

From Dolgelley I go up the twisting road through Drws-y-Nant towards Bala. By the little river as it rustles over boulder bed down to Dolgelley. Boulders rounded, great and small, left from the Ice Age and now stubborn to the ever-pushing stream. Up over watershed and to where the road slopes gently down to Bala. The way over the mountains, where road and railway are friendly.

Houses are lonely here set in the brown of the bracken and the fierce brightness of the summer flowers. Sheep graze the roadbanks and only the young lambs run from the coming car. The sound of the engine and the bleat of the horn are old sounds to the sheep and only the lambs jump away with kick of brown legs and whisk of uncut tail.

The tail-cutting is done when the lambs are growing. Done with shears or razor-sharp knife. The long white lengths are cut to a shortness to help against the maggots in the summer.

Lambing time in the spring when the shepherds are out all day and half the night. When the sheep-dogs take on a more anxious look and sit on haunches, watching the quick, gentle helping hands of the shepherd. A look, a feel, and the opinion made as to whether the ewe will want help or not. The hard, weathered hands of the shepherd gentle as a city nurse or studio painter. Only once in the while comes the hard case and it has to be the vet. The farm car is driven up the mountain track to the fold and there the ewe is placed on a folded sack on the back seat of the car; where on

market day the servant girl sits on her ride to market. Now the sheep is rushed into the village or the town where the vet has his brass-plated surgery and his three or four cars in the big garage, always waiting. A place of activity, with an assistant coming in from some distant call and then out again. Coming to collect some gleaming chromium instrument for cow calving or special testing.

The ewe is taken to the buildings behind the garage and there laid on a rubber-covered mattress. There college-trained hands and fantastic Inquisition-shaped instruments ease pain and do a successful lambing. Then the sheep is taken back to the farm.

Lambing time when new buds come and old snow memories are forgotten. And with the summer and the sunshine and the blue hills to look forward to.

Once sheep were hobbled. A crippling way to stop the climb of wall from one mountain run to the next. Now the sheep mix and there is a system of ear markings and body pitchings to prove the ownership of the animal.

The ears of the flock are marked in a certain way, dented nippings made and a record kept of the patterns. Patterns cunningly made so that if there should be sheep-stealing the mutilations of a new design shall be hard and a tell-tale change.

Pitching marks are made on the sides of the sheep after shearing time. Letters of the farm or the initials of the owner done in a monogram complication bought from the ironmongers. Or the simple letters cut out from an old tin and joined together and fixed to a wooden handle. The sheep are caught one at a time and taken to the pitching-shed. Here a pot of hot pitch is bubbling black, gurgling and spitting. And over the cauldron sits the farmer's wife, toil and trouble. A witch herself almost, as the coal and peat fire heats the pot set on the hearth built of old bricks. Red, and with the mortar still clinging.

The sheep are brought in and the metal branding-iron is dipped with a twist into the pitch. A tap on the pot side and then the farmer daintily lays the letters on the back of the sheep. A gentle press and the iron is lifted away before the pitch cools. The sheep is sent away across the yard, the next brought in.

The great black letters stark on the moving back. Clear and a witness of ownership. Winter snow and spring showers will wear away the pitch, the growing wool spread out the letters. So that by the summer shearing the shape of the letters will be gone and the wool will not be soiled.

And next year again will come the pitching. With the hands laying gentle the letters and by the pot will sit the wife to keep the black pitch bubbling.

Bala. To the chapel-goer this is the place where the ministers are trained. Here come the students heavy with B.A. or B.D., and with student days already only a memory.

Days at Aberystwyth and Bangor, Swansea and Cardiff gone for ever. No more Inter-Varsity Eisteddfodau with the Rag and Pranks; Blazers and Colours a sure excuse for nonsense.

Students come here for the last year of the training. A final last rub and polish. Sober already and on a Saturday neat in black suit and white collar and mourning tie on Bala Junction station. Waiting for the trains to go to all parts for the practice pulpit. Perhaps to Llanfechain or to Rhos the booked preacher has not come. The hurried postcard to say that he has gone elsewhere, to Liverpool or Birmingham with a better-paid Sunday. Send now to Bala. Bala will never let you down.

On a Saturday afternoon waiting for the trains, young men with the neat square cases, brown leather, black initialled. Edge of a pyjama caught sometimes in the quick packing, gay cloth untheological.

Twelve months at Bala College for the finer points of ministry. Voice training, throw your voice to the last pew, let it echo against the far wall, make that your sounding board.

And some Sundays they are at home, preaching in the College, before the Principal. All the year there is the Hope and the Wait. That some chapel will give them the "Call". Some pastorless church with the empty manse will summon them. The student young on trial, his best sermon in his inside pocket. A warm-hearted prayer learnt off straight and hymns picked for the swing and good fellowship of hearty singing.

The young ladies of Bala, it is said, marry mostly preachers. And widows with eligible daughters retire there.

Bala itself is a place with a tang in the air and a sleepiness about the houses, the people. The main street is wide, with lying dogs and old men spitting tobacco. Spit stained brown and a lick of the tongue to the wad in the cheek.

Bala with its Theological College and its lake.

One of the earliest Principals of the College was Thomas Charles, one of the founders of the Bible Society and an Oxford graduate and an ordained clergyman of the Church from the seventeen-seventies until 1811. In that year he founded the Cal-vinistic Methodist Church of Wales. This done out of disgust with the churchmen of his day. And now Charles of Bala is a name revered and honoured throughout Wales.

In the succeeding years of the last century bigotry and narrow-mindedness douched much of the initial fire and fervour which had given Welsh Nonconformity such a tremendous start in Wales. And this bigotry still exists in the country chapels controlled by the old, hard-working farmer deacons. The young people drift away from the countryside, forget the chapels.

But in the town chapels a new consciousness is rising among the wider-world deacons. The certain knowledge that the negative attitude is sending the chapels to a decline. And so the town chapels have a freer life, with social meetings and a gayer approach to the old religion. Yet in many of the country districts the old hardness remains.

It was from Llanfihangel y Pennant that Mary Jones walked to Bala to have a Bible. A long walk, the roads lonely. But at Bala the compensating kindness of Thomas Charles, who is buried in Llanycil churchyard out of Bala. The graveyard edge to edge with the cold waters of the lake. The wind blowing across the water, mountain fresh. With the clean rain and in winter the driving snow, piling up in long high drifts behind the tombstones. Smooth white mounds, dazzling in the moonlight like great starched shrouds. With rime on the old carved letters and pointed icicle and frozen tear on the headstones.

A place to pass quickly in the cold moonlight.

I stood on the lakeside road and looked through the trees to this lake in the centre of Wales. Bala Lake, over a thousand acres of blueness with the Dee trickling away at the bottom end. Ready to twist and wind in great gravel ox-bows down to Corwen and Llangollen and then on sullen and flat to Liverpool Bay. Starting in blueness and ending in mudflats and the fancy rainbow colours of the spilt oil.

Deep is Bala Lake. Glacial in origin but folklore says that Tegid's Palace is buried there. Llyn Tegid, the Welsh call Bala Lake. Tegid was an evil man, fond of singing and dancing and merrymaking. And he built a palace and only the harpist heard what the little bird said. That vengeance was coming, *so come away with me, harpist*. Up in the mountains the harpist looked down again and there was only his harp left floating on the new waters. The first waves making a sad tune against the strings.

A coldness about Bala Lake. A steel-blue efficiency as of a new unwrapped razor blade. Business-like and never much inviting the toy moment, the playing hour.

And there are the strange fish, the odd fish from the depths, the Gwyniad, or the White Fish, which float sometimes dead to the top. Fish never hooked by anglers' bait and never knowing the tussle of ever-pulling line. Shy fish these, and found only in the high lakes. Hating the light and floating dead to the surface. Handled by the curious hands, strange fish of Bala Lake.

A few trees around the lake but no clinging forest. People swim across in the summer and when the hard frosts come the sheep walk the ice, farm to farm. The thaw comes and the dogs help with the sorting and there is talk of wire netting for next year.

It was at Bala that Tennyson wrote parts of his "Idylls of the King", and in old days the town was famous for its knitting and its weaving. Once they had their knitting meetings when the harp was played and old songs sung, and goods knitted and money made. Business with pleasure; making gloves and woollen wigs.

George III had the rheumatic aches in his legs and was advised to wear black woollen stockings. These thought to be warmer and more beneficial than the usual silk hose. And these were supplied by Mr. Davies, a draper of Bala. Specially knitted, fine and dainty, by the daughter of a Trawsfynydd vicar.

The fine yarn stockings were sent from Bala to the Court drapers in London. Knitted in the ecclesiastical home in the Welsh mountains with the hope that the royal pains might go; twinge and creak of joint and leg be soothed away by the clinging warmth of Welsh wool.

To the west of Bala are the Aran mountains, distant misty, distant blue. At the foot of Aran Benllyn King Arthur is supposed to have spent his childhood. He who had in his court Merlin, who was entombed alive by the Lady of the Lake. Merlin, who was born in the fifth century to a vestal virgin and of a Roman father. And who was to be sacrificed by Vortigern so that blood could be laid on the site of his new fortress against the Saxons. But his knowledge of the Unknown and of Prophecy was so startling that his life was spared and he became the wisest of the bard magicians.

From a chapel I heard the singing. Perhaps this was some week-day prayer meeting or a rehearsal for the Singing Festival.

An exciting day is the Singing Festival. The chapels of the valley and the mountain come together. Come to sing hymns under some conductor, often a man from the singing valleys of South Wales.

And before the day there have been the rehearsals and the practices. The pipe organ or the harmonium overhauled and in fine song. Sometimes there is an orchestra, local musicians talented and amateur to accompany the singing.

The conductor stands impressive in the pulpit. The Bibles and the hymn books taken away and only a bare cloth there, with the small Festival hymn book, paper-covered and wrinkled.

Grand singing all in harmony with the last lines of the last verse repeated. A habit this, for if hwyl is raised, a thrilling emotion with the singing, then it is the custom not to end on the last line of the verse at the first time of singing. But to go on back halfway through the verse perhaps once or twice, perhaps three or four times, and the final ending with a reluctant Amen.

A thing looked forward to, the Singing Festival, by all the chapel people. After it the conductor is judged. And if found wanting then never again to come to the valley. But if the right man to raise the hwyl then he will be remembered and asked again. Come on this trip to the north for the three or four or five guineas pushed into his hand in a small folded envelope at the time of the handshake. Money passed as if not seen, a thing not to be mentioned.

Thrift, and a desire to be nice to people. These the characteristics of the North Welsh. And much of the criticism directed at the Welsh is on account of these two qualities.

For the thrift evolves to meanness and to a low standard of living in order to achieve the ambition of a fat bank balance. Rather than buy the comfortable chair, better to save the money. Better to live on the slate-floored back kitchen and save the best furniture in the front room. Better to leave the water to leak into the rubber boots or to try and repair with cycle patch than buy the new ones.

Eat bread and milk for tea for it is waste to buy the food in tins. And fish and bought jam are only for the preachers when they come to stay over Sunday.

The thrift becomes meanness. The old jaws of gold have their grip and there is no loosening. The days when living was hard and mountain farms gave only a poor income explain, perhaps, this thrift. And a desire for independence always, to pass on the farm intact from father to son. Little farm snug in the hollow of a mountain slope where the son was born, and from where he will go out on his bicycle some day to his first courting. And the sloping yard down which one day a father's coffin will be carried, the mourners watching the good neighbours who will be the bearers. Children will have played in the stunted garden at the front of the house, generations of them each in a make-believe world. This house and the land around is completly and utterly home; every stone and view and mood of weather is known and loved. This is what the exile Welshman remembers when he talks of his *hiraeth*. A sweet word that and meaning nostalgic longing, the bitter-sweet grief of remembrance.

The money in the bank is seldom invested except in real concrete things, such as the mortgage on a neighbouring farm. And on the weekly trip to market one of the first calls is at the bank. There a little written slip is passed across after the cheques have been paid in. The slip from the distant clerk across the broad, respectful counter, this paper with the balance written on it. The slip is taken home and in triumph shown to the wife in the rounded palm of the hand. A secret from the children, but a thing for boast.

The habit is hard to break off. But remember that the good generous heart is always there. Help for the neighbours at the time of harvest and cow calving. Help when trouble comes with death or a birth. And remember that the money is always freely lent to the poor neighbour who wants to send his boy or girl to the university or to the training college. Always the money for a "good cause", chapel-building or a missionary collection. Though here there is the printed list and a certain amount of competition.

The heart is good. The cup of tea always and the Welsh woman slips the eggs or the pound of butter into the English pocket with a "Sssh", a wagging, warning finger.

Perhaps this, after all, the ultimate salvation, the Kate good heart.

The desire to be nice to people, to be pleasant. The English talk of the shifty look, the downcast eye, the broken promise. A desire not to hurt people, and the promise is made to satisfy and to please when it is well known that it can never be kept. Times are mentioned and the plans are made, then forgotten. An impulsive nature to do things on the instant, full of tenderness and goodness.

They are my people. I am Welsh on both sides far, far back into the centuries. And my home is Wales. And perhaps I'm glad, too, that there is a gay irresponsibility still left after all the narrow-minded Nonconformity of the last century, and that the precious Celtic, impulsive, irresponsible heart is not lost.

III. THE PAINTED LINE, A SMUDGE, AND THE THREE VALES

THE PAINTED LINE, A SMUDGE,
AND THE THREE VALES

THREE fair valleys, beauty lands of Wales. And the holiday towns of the north coast, summery and lady painted. And the grey parts of Denbighshire and Flintshire where coal brought factories, and factories a litter of little houses, straight-rowed, numbered, empty-parloured, geranium-windowed.

A journey through the vales of Conway and Clwyd and Llangollen. Along the resorts and through industrial Wrexham.

Down the well-watered valleys and along the painted line of the sunshine towns. And a pause in the smudge where the coal has left grey towns, grey people.

I shall go through the farmlands watered by the Dee, constant talking as it plunges the boulder and rock channel through Llangollen. Through lovely Conway valley, river famous once for its pearls, with waters fast rising, fast flooding. Through the Vale of Clwyd, gentle sloped and with the quiet little towns and the prosperous farms. Through lands of water meadows, and rivers which the salmon climb with urge and fling up the weir walls. There where the poachers stand with quick-moving gaff in hand and a lad on a high tree to keep watch. This lad who watches the roads and the footpaths and the ways across the river fields. Ever on the watch for the water bailiff or the gamekeeper.

The shooting rights of the farms were once owned by the landlord. He coming to his shooting lodge, some Hall in a fertile nook of the hills kept empty except for the caretaker all the rest of the year. Then in the season the farmhands and the tenants' sons trained by the gamekeeper to do the beating and the gun carrying. Each day ending with a huge meal for all the helpers.

But many of the estates have now split up. Sometimes the tenants were given the chance to buy their own farms at a valuation. Or sometimes a syndicate bought up the whole estate and sold it piecemeal. The Hall becomes a guesthouse and the lodge at the main gate no longer sees to the opening of the carved white gate, for there some retired city man lives where once the head gardener came green-fingered home each night.

The shooting rights of the tenant-owned farms is now let off to the local hotel, or advertised through a solicitor and let to some new rich from a city. They who handle a double-barrelled gun in the same clumsy way as they handle a pitchfork. Never a quick rise to the shoulder and always firing though a bird be a rifle-shot away. And always, too, keeping the empty cartridge cases in the coat pocket and taking them back in the evening, witness of much noise.

Those from the village who go to help with gun carrying have learnt to stand just behind. For these men use a gun something like a golf club. And with a right-about turn at any noise from behind. Stray pellets rattle on thorn hedges and against the stone walls of the mountains. And in the airy game larders the birds hang, ready for the paying guests, killed by the straight, non-mauling shots of the gamekeeper.

My way will be along the towns of the North Wales coast, Prestatyn and Rhyl and Abergele, Colwyn Bay and Llandudno. Names made famous by the inches advert in the daily papers and where the sands are smooth and safe. And where there is a gay summer life. Colour and the prancing legs of the concert parties, the foot which flaps to the time of the music as Jill or Joe does the turn. A summer smile fixed, never to lengthen, never to cease. All for tired Lancashire, music from band and pier. At the railway station they climb stiff out of the arrival trains and on the other platforms those who have to go stand sadly staring. But Dad is pleased that it is all over and the pint in the home pub will be worth half a dozen in this place. And Mother hopes that the milk-man had the note this morning and that the pound is still safe under the flat heaviness of the china dog on the mantelpiece.

And I shall go to Wrexham and Flint and the other towns where people never come with high head and full pocket for the holiday. And where the only strangers who come with suitcase and paper bag are those home for the holiday. Home for mother's tea, this fortnight in the twelvemonth. For she bakes fresh fruit pies and makes the sweet scones which hold all the memories of childhood, and the ache of the little years gone by.

From Bala I go down with the young Dee, down to Corwen. Past grey, stone-built farmhouses with low hedges separating front gardens from farmyards. Bare, dull-green cabbage stalks before the latticed porch of the front door. And in the yard carts and implements and the rattling of chain as the barking dog strains out from the kennel.

Many of the farm dogs are treated badly. With no fixed meals and only the occasional scraps thrown. The dog is expected to help its own feeding by rabbit catching. Sometimes a dog becomes an egg-stealer and eats the newly-laid eggs from the poultry houses and the hen nests among the hay. The cure is always to uncap an egg and to empty. And then to fill with strong liquid mustard. The egg is put carefully down again and the thing is the joke of the week as the dog runs with licking jaws to the cooling rain tub.

On the road to Corwen, past little larch coppices and the heavier, quieter darkness of fir plantations. There where all green elves and the little people of the green trees must live and watch all who pass by on the road through the valley.

Under the gloom of Penypigyn mountain lies Corwen. Here where Owain Glyndwr once lived and where he is still something of a show-piece, a persistent relic. Associations pointed out and the places where he came and went are hallowed, almost. His name, Glyndwr, said to be taken from Glyndyfrdwy, near Corwen. Glyndwr had a home, too, at Sycharth, near Llangedwyn in the Tanat valley.

Glyndwr fought against the English. He was something of an egotist and loved the idea of himself as the King of Wales. And perhaps he was a little hasty in his destruction of buildings.

Owain Glyndwr lived regally. A bard records that at his palace were signs of rare eating and fine living. Whether it is the palace at Sycharth or Glyndyfrdwy to which the bard refers is not known. But we hear that the mansion had nine halls and in each was a wardrobe. And for those who came to stay with the King of Wales there was accommodation in a guesthouse.

In the palace was a pigeon-house and a warren. And there were fish ponds for fresh fish and a heronry for game and sport. The palace had its own mill, its own orchard and its private vineyard.

The pomp is gone and grass grows where the vines were raised tender. And the orchard is forgotten, but perhaps its fine trees still grow in some hedgerow. For in that way is the home of Owain de Galles, who lived near Llansantffraid, in that way is his orchard remembered. An old twisted sweet apple tree strangely lonely in a hedge of neat thorn and flexing ash.

Perhaps cattle now push mud in the fish pond of Glyndwr's palace and spring lambs bounce where once the welcome guesthouse waited hospitable.

Owain fought the losing battle and the King of England became Lord of Wales also. And London palace swells London pride and only the bard records the warren and the pigeon-house, the orchard and the vineyard. These which once the King of Wales raised for his royal pleasure.

On the tree-lined road out from Corwen I passed a great cart mare. Not in the working harness with the sweat in white foam on the leather edges. Or with the long guiding rein cords from the ploughing wrapped into a neat bundle and dangling yellow on the great collar.

But a dressed horse, a most wonderfully dressed horse. With fantastic gay ribbons flapping in the breeze. Red and white and blue and green and yellow. In long, dancing lines and done up in great bunches on tail and mane. A great twinkling and tingling of brasswork, yellow plate on the flat parts of this best harness. Catching the June sunlight as it came in cathedral shafts through the west window openings of the trees.

A little man was leading the horse by a pure white halter. His hands old and worn against the bright new rope. And the rims of the best black jacket showing beyond the sleeves of a white overall, the buttons open and the loose parts of the coat flapping back. Whipcord breeches with a "wheep-wheep" as he walked, the sound plainly heard above the clip-clop of the moving horse. Best breeches, and below, the yellow felt leggings worn by the older farm workers in Wales. A kind of soft skin, of fawn yellow, and buttoning up the one side with brown pearly buttons.

His one hand up to the halter. His other hand stiff by his side. And in that straight hand the great square of cardboard held, with the words in red letters and blue shadow to say FIRST PRIZE and then the name of the horse printed in blue-black ink BRONWEN.

The first prize in the show had gone to Bronwen. And the card said more, that the prize was not only for the best-dressed horse but for the best all-rounder. Best coat and limb and stand. But why this name for a horse, why not some little name like Bet or Jane or Sal? Oh, but there was a story.

The boss had had a little girl called Bronwen. The T.B. had got into her bones and she had just withered away. So the boss had spent all the guineas to get the best cart mare in the county, getting her from some great sale in the English shires. Bringing her all the way here in a special horse-box and even rebuilding the stable for her. And, of course, calling this perfect healthy mare Bronwen. And there was not a mare who could touch Bronwen in any of the shows. *She's in a class of her own.*

Up the road they went, this wagoner and Bronwen. The mare in a great blaze when the sunshine caught them. And in the shadows the ribbons and white flapping coat and the prize card could be seen clear.

The agricultural shows thrive. A field outside the town or village is taken and there a wire ring set up. Marquees and stands and stalls. Competitions for the best stock of all descriptions, for the best garden and agricultural produce. And competitions for horse jumping and games on horseback, for trotting matches and for galloway races. And sometimes now they bring in the motor cycle racing and foot sports.

The child and her T.B. This one had the romantic story, but in every parish, almost, there are the families *who have it in them*. For the country people believe that it is hereditary and that a baby is born full or free of it.

In earlier days the T.B. pruned off one or more in the larger families. Those living in damp, mist-lingering valleys, and the under-nourished of large families on tiny holdings. Little places where the rent was always a struggle and a worry all the year. So that food for the children was often insufficient, and the bulk of the milk had to go towards the butter-making. And even if the disease was known there was no money towards proper treatment.

Even now in these healthier times tuberculosis is a worry in the villages. And I can remember the ones of my own age who had the blackness under the eyes and a faint greenness there. The thinning face and a way of leaning against a humming telephone post or a gay creeper-covered stone wall with the coughing. They who in due course were taken away to the sanatorium. Who came back again, bright with the constant hope. And who lived in tents and in wooden shacks in the gardens where the wind and the breezes came off the fields and the mountains. One, with fight in his blood, going to live in the shade of a fir wood, for the trees were supposed to be good for this thing. Another who said that he had learnt a way of breathing and that all would be well. Another who put his faith in church and prayer and walked there, a little slower each day with his halting sticks.

But the time came young to all of them, and fir wood and shack and special breathing and even the hand of God himself had no way of stopping the end.

They died, one at a time over the years. And we followed behind them to the cemetery on the bare hillside, or to the village church-yard shaded with the beech and the elm trees. We followed them sadly and a little frightened and not understanding quite why it should have been them and not us.

We were glad to get away from the bleak cemetery, where the chapel people are buried and where the wind whistles and hums in the narrow, pointed, iron railings which surround the place. And from the churchyard where summer and winter the leaves seem to drop, with a laugh at autumn. Coming down, one or two, taunting green in the summer. Or in January, the last half-dozen left over from autumn gradually falling yellow and withered as the rooks caw in the taller elms at the back of the vicarage garden. The little gate through which the Vicar comes, serene in his robes. In the wet weather with an umbrella or in the cold months with the addition of a black overcoat.

The gate through which he would go at the end of it all. Hurriedly and quickly and seemingly as glad as all of us to get away. To tea and bright fenders and toast, things to drive away fear and too much thought of the luck of life.

I go on through the Dee valley, on to Llangollen. First I came here, long ago, unromantic on the railway.

Railway stations, tiny halts or great echoing halls. Open to the sky or with glassy roofs. Places of soot and grimed hands of noise and great welts of steam.

But the small country stations catch all the romance of the railway. The line of lighted yellow windows and the great flare as the fire-box red swings open. Glowing faces and arms overalled blue. The crash of closing doors, the green wave and sharp, short whistles.

Llangollen has the station by the river. The platform with the one edge to the bright steel rails and the other railed above the deep to the water of the Dee river. Racing and twisting, a white cataract of a river. Smooth water meeting bed boulder and the grand spray rebellion. Foam and bubble and annoyed anxious water hurrying on. A grand first view of Llangollen and a place to gaze over the railway and watch dizzy the water, and only the tickets to be handed in and the cases heavy to remember that this is a holiday only.

They call the narrow valley of Llangollen the Vale. Call it that in the guide books modern and the old English Esquired guides. And old and new agree to its beauty. The Dee, salmoned and trouted, wooded and gravel-bedded, with the great water meadows and the rich, good farms. Pastoral rising to the sides of the valley, the hills half majestic mountain. On the one side the broken, nature-quarried Eglwyseg rocks, pink and white in the sunshine, wild and grey in winter dullness. Rocks loose and shaled and the sheep wandering, from rich grass to sudden rock.

The other side of the valley has the hill rising steep, and topped with the spidery trees and the lonely Roman road.

And by Eglwyseg rocks the rising heights of Castell Dinas Bran, Crow Castle. The arched castle ruin scraggy on the mountain top. Black against the sunset and haunted with all the memories of life lived full and sweet. This castle, Tibetan, perched with the view of the blue miles. Dangerous view into England, wait for the glint of arms. And with the view green into Wales. A disturbing relic, Castell Dinas Bran. A ruin left nightmared and carved from a great bad dream, grotesque and dwarfish. Much of its story is shy in history. But the tale told of lovely Welsh Myfanwy Fechan who in the fourteenth century lived in this wild top of a place, this house on a hill. And she had a lover, one Hywel ap Einion Llygliw, and the love story remains. How he climbed the steep mountain each night with a song and verse.

Llangollen Bridge is one of the Wonders Seven of Wales. Built by a fourteenth-century bishop and carrying all the chrome cars and the heavy tractors safely to-day. And tested not only with the wheels and the stamping feet but by the Dee when Bala Lake swims over and the river is muddy yellow. Spouting on each side of the stout arches, with white, broken sticks, spinning, floating.

Always a place for the travellers, Llangollen, Wordsworth head up to Dinas Bran and writing his *Ruins of a Castle in North Wales*. And the famous Hand Hotel where came many of the famous ones. This hostelry with its yard to the Holyhead road. Where the stage-coaches came wheeling in with crack of whip and grate of wheels on gravel. The cars turn in now and rest with the creak of cooling engine and the smell of hot oil. No more the teams of horses, impatient and pawing on a frosty morning ready for away. The ostlers with clapping hands and blowing finger-nails. The hot punch stirred with the great curved spoon and passengers taking the last warm drink. Rime on the coach windows and the tin baggage boxes have frozen tears, transparent and cold.

The Royal Hotel, too, with its walls straight to the Dee and its garden by the waters.

The people of Llangollen make commerce of their beauty. *Souvenirs from Lovely Llangollen*. And the great revolving racks of postcards, pretty views for auntie in Manchester. We've walked there, there just where I've put the cross.

Something of an industry, this catering for the visitors. They who dress differently, always. With shorts and the tweed skirts, the cord trousers and the deerstalker hats. The locals always respectful to them, showing them the way to the beauty spots with pointed finger and flexing wrist.

I stand on the bridge at Llangollen, hands on the grey stone, and watch the river bed, black rock through the moving water. Try to remember the yesterdays when Owain Glyndwr lived in the valley, ten miles up at Corwen. He the hero of the last great struggle for independence for Wales, constant in his bickerings and fightings with the English. Yet marrying all his daughters to full-blooded English gentry.

And the Ladies of Llangollen, what of them? Of Lady Butler and the Hon. Mrs. Ponsonby and their servant, Mary Carrol. The Honourable and the Lady and the Servant now mingle dust in one grave. These ladies eccentric living at Plas Newydd and in touch with the great ones of the day, with the Duke of Wellington and with Scott and with Wordsworth who all stayed at the house. The home remains, neat and tidy and very old, with a caretaker and the visitors curious. Tourists walk the lawns and peep into the glen, as if expecting to see the Ladies there.

For half a century in sweet devotion the ladies lived together. Never sleeping away from Plas Newydd and visited by the great ones of the time. Mr. Wordsworth wrote a touching poem for them and the callers were usually on their way to Holyhead and to Ireland. The house is now open to the public and is a great magpie of a place, black and white. With carvings on the outside like gnarled warts and all cellophane fresh and very respectable.

Within sound of the Dee I found the blacksmith's shop. Walking a twisting side street by the edge of the river and I smelt the burning hoof; heard the talking of man to horse. And after that the clang and tinkle of an anvil.

The smell and the talking and the noise of the anvil bringing young days back to me. When I used to spend the days of my summer holiday in the blacksmith's shop near to my old home set in the orchard and the walnut trees.

This blacksmith's shop of my youth had been a lonely place, too. With no village street and the only constant noise the hurried bubble of a brook against the one brick wall of the smithy. The smith had suffered from asthma and I would go into the shop to find all quiet except for the drowning breath of the old man, lonely now that his son, who had been his striker, had gone away to the works in the Midlands. The kind old man sitting on the very anvil itself and on his knees a flat, rusted piece of iron. And in the iron a little burning cone of some special herb, a relief for the asthma. And at such times my duty always was to pump a little at the bellows to keep the fire going. That and to build a fresh cone of the powder on another old piece of iron, ready for when the little pyramid he was inhaling had burnt away to white, useless ash.

But Llangollen now, and the smithy of my boy days has become a cattle-shed. Cows to stand and spiders to run where once iron was shaped cunningly, and old farm tools were made new again.

Here a blacksmith's shop with its smell of burnt hoof, the sizzle of hot iron on carefully-trimmed foot. Or the clanking of anvil, thumps of the hammer on the shaping iron and the clinks as the hammer bounces free on the anvil in between the heavy, aiming blows. Sparks upward, bright against the leather apron. Or lost, burnt falling stars to the bricked floor. Shoes and farm implements made and still sometimes the iron rim to be put on the wooden wheel of a farm cart. Though often now, when one great wheel breaks, the other is unloosed and leant in retirement against some outbuilding wall. And the bouncing pneumatic wheels are fixed, rubber-tyred from some old car. To run smooth with no great heavy wooden, iron-shod wheel to turn. Quiet and hardly a whisper these modern wheels, hardly a squeak behind the horse.

But still, sometimes, comes the day when in the village comes the co-operative job. Blacksmith and carpenter join, individualism interwoven for an afternoon. A harmony and an easy working between them. The grunts and the half-said words in Welsh at the time of the rim-fixing.

The village carpenter has made the wooden wheel. A man of great versatility, who makes the coffins and undertakes all the organisation of a country funeral from last rites to arranging with the monumental masons for the white marble tombstone. Or who can make all the doors and rafters, skirting boards and the stairs for a new house. Or who, in a delicate way, can lay aside trade and bring craft to his finger-tips and make the carved milking stool, or the cabinet to hold the gramophone records.

And he is a wheelwright, too, that strange, clever craft of hubs from heart of oak, and spokes, and round smooth rims. Little wheels for the small mill lorry, or great head-high wheels for an old-fashioned hay wagon. A hay wagon wheel which will be painted a gay yellow and green and red, so that in the old tradition the wheels may be a blaze of colour, dazzling as they turn in the sunshine.

The wooden wheel made, comes the time of fixing the iron rim, safe and never to bowl away loose from the wheel down some steep hill. Never to clank in frosty weather or to be too tight in the wet weather; with the rain coming and a buckle as the wood swells.

A job for the blacksmith and for the carpenter. The wheel is taken to the blacksmith's shop. There laid on a round bed of iron, carefully and gently. In the morning the blacksmith will have had the measurements and made an iron band of the right diameter exactly when cold. The wheel is brought to the smithy in the afternoon and the iron band is made red hot. It expands and slips easily over the rim of the wheel. Comes now the difficult part. Blacksmith and carpenter hold the iron rim on the wheel in the exact position with long pincers, faces turned away from the heat. Then the blacksmith's striker comes with buckets of water which he throws over the hot metal. A steam and the smell of hot iron turned suddenly cold. The iron shrinks, clings to the edge of the wheel. The rim is on. A bowl along to see that it runs true.

The blacksmiths' shops are closing in North Wales, with the older men dying and no apprentices to take over the craft. The striker gone to the quarries or to drive some lorry. The double doors before the shoeing-shed are closed, and the shop itself has cobwebs brave and new across the once red-coke hearth. The great leather wrinkles of the bellows are stiff and a pull at the long, polished handle brings a groan, a creak and a rise of dust from the once water-filled cooling tank around the nozzle. Under the hearth the cooling vat is red with rusty water, here where once the hot new-made shapes were dipped at the end of the tongs for the quick cooling. The shine on the anvil has gone and the supporting tree stump sags and sinks and leans away. But a propelling pencil tapped on it gives the ring, and all the old bounce and spring are still there. Around the wall, quiet on nails, hang all the strange instruments. Tools for iron cutting and for twisting, which with hands and heart and fire could make the ornamental gates, the rows of fancy fencing. A dust now, the bags of nails going to rust and no impatient paw of horse on the cobblestones in the shed. Outside once they pasted up a notice, that this place was for sale, tools and goodwill and the building, everything. But there were no offers and the man who wanted it for a garage changed his mind. Said that it was no good and that there was no place for cars to draw up. No place to wait for petrol.

The village carpenters' shops still flourish, for undertaking is an essential business. And a new roof to a barn is wanted often and there is no quick way to make rafters and joists for an eighteenth-century building. Gates are still made of timber, and any time comes the order to make a new trailer for a farmer's car. This to take the pigs to market or to bring home the bought, pedigree sheep. And the carpenter still makes a shed for the tractor, of galvanised iron on a wooden frame.

Up in the mountains haystacks and corn ricks are still thatched. There in the hills where they cannot spare the building for too much fodder and corn storage. And where the mania for sudden, soon threshing has not reached. Long straw stalks are used for the thatching, or coarse long brown rush. One length overlaying the next and all pegged down with rough twine. This a wonderful waterproof; and a rick well thatched will last all snow and rain.

Basket-makers still weave, and grow osiers in specially cultivated patches in back-garden streams. Stripping the pliable stems, and the peeled bark thrown away. The stems are dried and in time the butter baskets are made, or the fruit hampers. And once in a while a fancy dog basket is made for some visitor. She who wants it for sentimental reasons. Not knowing the bargain and that this white basket will last when the brown-varnished gilded affairs have split open and the twigs have been used for morning fire.

I have met, too, an old man, a great white beard of an old man, who goes from farm to farm in North Wales sharpening saws. A strange way of earning a living, but with his little pack of tools he can sharpen any saw. From a tiny hand affair to the great, dangerous circular saws deep in humbled sawdust.

A good place for the old craftsmen, Merionethshire and Caernarvonshire and the other remote North Wales counties. A land where machine tools are only talk brought home from the wars by prodigal son and factory daughter. And now the son has two horses and an awkward stoney field to plough. And the daughter remembers the Midland factory hostel only dimly, what with all the butter to make; all the calves to feed.

On east from Llangollen to the near Border. Along the road above Llangollen Vale with its view in the distance of the wooded flat lands of the English plain.

The road from out of the lovely valley to the first of the factory land with the black chimneys at Acrefair.

And coming towards me the gleam and the colour of a row of motor coaches. Heads and waving hands from the half-down side windows and a great cheer for me as coach after coach in the half-dozen goes by with draught and blue lingering exhaust.

Some Sunday school trip, a thing which comes once a year. All the chapels of the village perhaps joining together and forget all the old roots back to Calvin and Wesley. A day is fixed for the trip and the organising committee will have been at work. Three from each chapel with much planning and reporting to the Sunday schools. And sometimes there is a village where the church joins in as well. So that on the appointed day all people of religion will have left the village. And the only remaining ones will be the heathens, and those who are sick in the body as well as those who are sick in the soul. The heathens will not be allowed to come, those who, when the time comes, will be buried as plainly and as simply as possible. Perhaps in the village are one or two Catholics, life is one long seaside trip for them, so say the chapel people, what with so much pleasure and so much sin in their lives. They must not be allowed to come on any account, they who love crosses and forgiveness of sins.

The night before the trip day there is much listening to weather forecasts, much studying of barometers. Tapping of glass and anxious watching of the needle. The old people hold fingers up to the first stars for the feel of the wind. Cock heads and listen to whether the sunset wind moans or sings in the hedgerows. And they watch to see if the sun sinks red-faced and ready for a happy to-morrow, or whether he goes down peevish with threat of rain and summer storm.

Trip day comes. The children wake late, for sleep came hard in the thrill of last night. The old people wake first, satisfied as always with their few hours. Fires are lit and kettles sing and rattle lids at half-past six in the morning. Vacuum flasks are taken down from the harvest shelf and washed out. Big lid-full pots of tea are made. Sandwiches are cut; red with tomatoes and sticky with jam. Cakes are sliced and Swiss rolls tenderly wrapped. Bottles of lemonade are corked and tied down with string, a sharp defiance of the company who say that this bottle is their property and must not be used for any other drink whatsoever. But who wants to take company drinks to the seaside when every house in the village can brew nettle beer and make tanged lemonade for the children?

At nine o'clock the buses come groaning empty up the street. Come from the garage in town and on market day used for the hourly service. But no baskets to go on the railed top and the racks inside are for food and spades and buckets only. No one to-day will dare to talk the price of eggs or the bad sale of store cattle.

The buses load; the drivers, cigaretted, lean over and watch the shouting and the challenging who's to sit by who.

All in and the coloured coaches drive away and the sad ones who have to stay, they stand and wave until the last broad-backed bus has rounded the corner.

God's people gone to the seaside. Cheerio, with best suit and money to burn, this one day. Rhyl or Llandudno, or perhaps the younger ones have had their way this year and it is far-away Southport or Blackpool after all. A long ride to a sunny place, and it's only on the way back home that the hymns will be sung, the gay holiday bus become a chapel on wheels, hurrying home to Wales.

A grey town, Wrexham. With the pitheads around it and the shadow days of the distressed area still lingering in this, the largest North Wales town. A wonderful steepled church here and a football ground where they play international.

A gayness come to Wrexham at the time of the international football matches. Rosettes and rattles and hand-bells, noise for the making. Football fills the mind, and watching is more important than playing. Form and the referee talked bare and pubs hear what should have been and what next time must be remembered.

Yale, who founded the U.S.A. university, is buried in Wrexham churchyard. Elihu Yale has a good church to keep him company. Its bells are toned joyful as if ever full of Christmas and weddings and wars ended. In the last light of day I have heard the practice pealing crashing sweet and wonderful over the town. The church tower red with reflected sunset and all the carving on it like ivy stems growing to some ordered system.

The town is of Saxon origin and the church was built at the end of the fifteenth century.

A grey town with a grey spirit. Old buses in the streets and the tired-faced miners in black rows along the windows.

In the quiet back streets the early-evening clap of clogs. A romantic moment of Holland, stage set in the mind with great wide trousers, the gay patches, the neat wooden clogs. A filled, happy theatre, dancing curtains, cigarette haze in the house lights. But a memory only. The clogs in the streets outside are black with coal dust. The cap is grey and pulled down low over one ear where the wrinkles are black. The hurried pithead bath and only the great reaches of the body washed clean. A black ridge, too, under

the worried eyes. The man looks up and the blackness of the holes
of his nostrils bulge open as he sniffs. The miner walks on again,
his clogs beating time into the distance. Steady and faint and far
away, this undertaker of our time up from the earth.

I go back into my room, draw the evening curtains. The firelight dances bright on the great brass rings. And in each curved
metal there is a reflection of the gay fire in my room, the gay
pictures on my wall.

Outside, other clogs are coming, other feet tramping home.

Wrexham still has the memory of the bitter sadness of the long
dole queue days. The shuffling outside the Labour, the pencil tight
on the end of the chain, the dirty counter and the wasted morning.

Around the town are the mining villages, Rhos and Gresford
and the rest. Rhos which is brim-full of singing and where they
get the big choirs and the orchestras.

Sweet and famous are the bells of Gresford. Once the Wonders
Seven of Wales and in that lovely list came the glad ring of the
bells of Gresford Parish Church. Sweet church bells with marriage
call across the meadows. Or the mourning bell, worried and
steady.

Sextons once used to sell grease from the church bells. This supposed to be a cure for the ringworm, consecrated and a certain
healing.

A lake, too, at Gresford. Set in any other frame would make a
great pond. Dull and scum surfaced or with the slow waddle of
farm geese or Christmas ducks at the muddy sides. But Gresford
pool is a lovely lake. Bordered by the village road and clear with
the reflection of loved houses, homes by the mere side.

And in winter there is the skating. Grand country skating with
frosty stars and a great cold moon. North Wales skating is not on
the mountain lakes but only in the valleys. On the Border canal or
on village pond. Farm lads slide with great hob-nailed boots,
scratching and tearing at the clear ice, clear with the green water
weeds below, unwaving and still. Ice with the white air bubbles
and a crack as the weight comes and new strains are placed on
the complaining water.

Only the upper ones of the parish skate. The Schoolmaster, the
Vicar and the Doctor. Those who have been to college and learnt
to glide on these awkward steel blades.

With the coming of the frost farmers make plans for the outdoor
feeding of the wintering cattle. Hardy young bullocks who stay
out the winter with hedge and bank for shelter. And up in the
mountains the shepherds will round up the lambing sheep to make
certain that no young, wet-born lamb will freeze to death if the

mother dies. The cold wind of crag and stone untempered to the young and the foot-stamping, warm-breathing ewe the only protection.

And on the Border and in the valleys men climb up to garret, to box room and to lumber loft. There where the apples are stored, the old broken beehives, and the croquet hoops bought with the house. Up there in the dust and where the frost makes fantastic patterns on the skylight and where black spiders run, stay sudden still. And where all the four seasons' memories are stored away. Apple and blossom time; the broken lawn mower, the small-cut grass still brown and dry on the blades; the great red pot which held the Christmas tree always before the children grew up, died to the bugle or just sailed away; and the old skates like a brace of brown birds hung from the rusty hook. The legs of black leather oiled and supple and dull with grease. And the blades like great sharp beaks grown long and dream-like. Old, old-fashioned skates. With a flat wooden base and a great protruding screw on the heel. And straps looping through at the front.

Skates from the old days, kept new and fresh with oil on the straps, grease on the blades. Taken down from the lumber room at this time of frost. Stiff clerical climbing, or white medical hands smoothing the blade clear and clean, or the Schoolmaster with the memory of 'varsity days, late Victorian, gay Edwardian. Climbing down with skates in hand, for the ponds have frozen again and the great cold has come to North Wales.

Old special boots are found on the last forgotten rack of the boot cupboard, or dangling by the laces behind some seldom-opened door.

And the farm lads slide and laugh and Welsh swear words echo the ice in the late afternoon, the last half-hour before the milking starts. And the boys of the village come with old boxes, old chairs, and rusty sledges. And the cowman stands on the last inches of ground, his feet leaving the certain shapes in the crinkled white-frost grass, and with the old pole he breaks the ice for the cattle to drink. Then the skaters of the village screw on the skates to heel of shoes, a first hole made with an awl, for the leather has shrunk with the years. They fasten the straps round the toe and carry the skates and the shoes across the hard, echoing ground of the meadows and under the winter stillness of the high thorn hedges.

A shout comes from the pond. The skates are coming, the first of the skates. A thrill comes to the small boys, the ice must be safe.

Then other skaters come. The cowman takes home the cows from the water to the night milking. The farm workers leave for the cattle feeding and to help with the milking. The small boys go home for the tea and shout to each other that they'll be back in the moonlight.

On the ice the skaters wheel and cut and turn. Old forgotten tricks and ways coming back again. The falls and the laughter and the grating ring as steel cuts ice, sharp and certain.

And with the darkness someone fetches the storm lanterns. Four of them, yellow, and the paraffin burning jagged on the uneven wicks. The lanterns are set one at each side, and one at each end of the pool. The lantern glass is reflected long and far away in the marked, cut ice. And sometimes the wind that comes with the moonlight tinkles the wire handle, the noise heard only in the moments between the talk and the laughter and the scream and rake of the skates.

Others come from the next parish which has no pond; or those on holiday. Or those from the village who just want to stand on the ice in the moonlight. Walk where they can only walk once or twice in the twelvemonth. And where perhaps to-morrow will be water again, with a lap and a pattern in the first warm wind of spring.

From Wrexham I come back to Llangollen again. Pause and listen to the Dee, and then on to the sacred place, two miles north-west of Llangollen where is Valle Crucis Abbey, Cistercian House founded in 1200 by Madoc ap Gruffydd Maelor and dissolved in 1535. The abbey stands in green meadows by a small stream. Tranquil and very serene with the heights of the building still safe. Unhurried hours remembered under the high walls. The years of worship not forgotten, and the abbey still a sacred place. Though there is no notice-board outside and no gay wayside pulpit to catch the passers-by as they go up the road ready for the steep, sweet air of the Horse Shoe Pass. The meadow around the abbey has no weathered tombstones and the mounds have been levelled with the years. But we do not plough this field, says the farmer, we could not disturb their bones. So the same grass roots grow as have been all the centuries, with no ploughing, no re-seeding. Never the yellow corn to bend the long stalks, never the rustle of oats and the rub of barley in the wind, never the heavy heads of full wheat. Never the swing of sickle, the pound of self-binder. Never a fresh furrow damp and crow followed. With root crops and straight rows of turnips, swedes and beet. But a pasture always, this meadow by the abbey, and they sleep well under the green.

But they built their abbey weak at first, the builders of Valle Crucis. For the foundations were not strong enough and the building was in danger of a collapse.

In all the Cistercian abbeys a lamp was always kept burning before the altar. And Valle Crucis had its little window in one wall so that the sacristan could see through and keep watch that the flame was alight.

In the last century the inside of the abbey was excavated. And there was found a vast number of human bones, which were buried again.

From Valle Crucis Abbey the road rises steep to the mountains and the Horse Shoe Pass. The watered lands of the monk farmers left behind and the road bending up over the hills and to the Vale of Clwyd. From the green fields of the valley of Llangollen and the hedgerows thick and old and well made, the valley well wooded, up to the air of the mountains. The grass shorter and the rocks bare through the thin soil. Sheep grazing and balancing from perch to perch to find fresh, sweeter grass. The gorse and the heather and the shy hiding bilberries. Black crimson fruit under the green leaves. And the ground with a spring in it, the air with a tang.

The pass is shaped like a horse-shoe, a road around a bowl in the mountains. Climbing steep all the way with twists and turns in the giant curve. The one side an edge of mountain to the blue sky and the white drifting of the summer clouds. Stare up and the clouds stand still and it is the heather-top hill which is sailing quiet and giddy with the steady wind. Look down the drop to the narrow valley, the houses like toy farms on a nursery floor, the dizzy distance with the smoke of tiny chimney and the fields in handfuls.

The cars go up and down with the groaning, low-geared engines and summer drivers serious in the bright family car. *Dad, are your brakes tested and safe?* One skid, one drop, one last cart-wheel.

Up and down, and watching from the bottom they seem slow lizards, glinting snails in the sunlight.

In the winter the snows here are deep and the pass whines with blizzard. In the valley roads the cars rattle with clanking snow chains, a slip only into the ditch or a soft thorn hedge. But on the pass there can be no slipping and only the daring venture the slow climb, the long descent.

Time was when the hearse, black and sedate, met the white blizzard on the top of the pass. The snow drifting in smooth billows and the edge of the road lost in dangerous softness. The hearse and the coffin left and an anxious wait for the thaw to come and the funeral to go on.

A funeral in North Wales is an event, a social occasion. Men in each parish who are almost professional mourners, going in black suit and hard bowler hat on bike and train to funerals for miles round. Always, too, the food in the chapel vestry, the relatives paying and a death in the family a treasured thing. Once the spiced ale and cakes. Now the cups of tea and the sandwiches sardine.

On the moors by the Horse Shoe Pass I saw the white lengths of the beehives. Straight against the redness of the heather, neat and with the military sameness. Some local bee-keeper had taken his hives up to the heather so that he might have the special honey. This Welsh bee-master who had arranged with the landowner and had taken his hives there on some hired lorry and there opened the little sliding doors of the hive. And the bees had come out among the little crimson flowers of the heather.

Most of the North Wales villages have at least one bee-keeper. The man to hive swarms and a man with honey and wax for sale. Honey for the housewife and wax for the local saddler or tailor to wax threads. Or for the old-fashioned ladies who still use bees-wax and turpentine to polish floors and furniture. The ladies who say that there is no polish so good and that the smell is healthy and that the shine lasts ten times longer than the fancy, easy stuff bought in a bottle.

Once the bees were kept in straw skeps, and all the bees had to be killed with smoke before the honey could be extracted. But all is organised now and profitable. Except when the diseases come. I can still remember the thrill of hot summer days when the bees had swarmed. My father and I climbing green, cool, apple trees to some thin, waving top branch. Big and moving with the football weight of the bees heavy laden with honey. And bees crawling over my bare knees. A grand buzz and a new hive to add to the long row under the big thorn hedge at the top of the garden.

Down from the Horse Shoe Pass and my way is the Vale of Clwyd.

The Vale of Clwyd, called that, by its own people. Not a name fancy and poetical for the exiles or the office guide-book man. But an area accepted by that name and never a thought for the poetry or the tempting word. A rich, green valley, facing north to the sea and backed at the south by the mountains, with gentle sloping sides.

Coming down from the heights of the Horse Shoe Pass to a lush valley of good farms, neat with stacks and well-kept orchard houses. Great apple and pear and plum trees, waving blossom in spring time, white and pink, and late frost the only enemy. With the summer the blossom falling and an untidiness coming. The pigs rooting in between the trees and turning muddy the dainty fallen petals. And while the hay is being gathered in and the corn ripens, then the apples thicken and a juiciness comes to the pear. The green plums swell and turn Victoria pink or dusty blue. A bloom comes and the wasps, and after that the gathering. Some of the apples stored in garrets for the winter, laid carefully on old sheets of newspaper or in boxes begged from the grocer. Some of the apples are sold to the produce lorries which come around once a week with dialled scales and pocket ready reckoner and flipping wallet. Pears sold, soft Williams and the hard little Christmas pears which will soften with keeping. The plums fill the giant wicker clothes baskets with lumpy red and blue and egg-yellow. The dealer picks out the one or two and rubs with his finger to see if the bloom is still on the small, red-stoned damsons and the big, luscious Czar plums.

A few only kept back for the bottling, for stewing, for jamming. Enough for the winter, sell any surplus. An itch in the Welsh to turn produce into hard cash. Even the snowdrops from under the beech trees on the lawn, even the violets blue and white from the sidewalks of the garden. Daffodils and narcissi left hardly a day, golden and red-fringed white, between the whitewashed trunks of the apple trees. All picked and sold fresh. Big, nodding bundles, dropping yellow pollen at a shake of the hand. And with the cut stalks oozing out the stickiness, white blood of the sad daffodils.

I've seen them, I've helped to pick them, these hampers full of beauty. What's a lovely orchard for but to make money? Money to put in the bank and all help towards the ultimate aim of the thousand pounds saved. March along and rattle the money-boxes, live in the stone-flagged kitchens and keep the comfortable parlour spick and span and unused except when the preacher comes to stay. Or when the daughter brings home the English husband, man of easy-worn suits and wasteful cigarette ash.

But this beautiful Vale of Clwyd, marcher land once of Lord Grey de Ruthyn, bitter particular enemy of Owain Glyndwr. This Vale watered by the Clwyd river in its thirty miles to the sea. The river rising south-west of red-grey Ruthin and joined below St. Asaph by the River Elwy. The two together to the sea, fresh Vale water lost in busy Liverpool Bay.

Quiet towns, Ruthin and Denbigh and St. Asaph. And a balmy air about the Vale of Clwyd. A place to relax in, with three score and ten a certainty if there be no flood or fire or pestilence. With the sea near for those hardy enough for the holiday coast towns. But there are the sides of the Clwydian Hills, soft places to find a peace.

Denbigh was famous once for its boot- and glove-making and these were supplied in quantity to London.

And in Denbigh there once lived an old woman who had the method of telling the sex of an unborn child. She who held a shoulder-blade of mutton before a hot fire until it was scorched and brittle enough for her to put her hag's thumbs through.

Through the holes she had made she threaded thin string carefully and first time sure. Then she suspended this blade by the string above the back door, allowing it there to dangle.

And the first to enter next morning, excepting regular members of the household, man or woman, would be of the sex of the child who was yet to be born.

Something of a witch she must have been, this evil one of the last century. She toasting her black knees before a good fire with the sheep's blade in her hands held to the bars. Turning it round and sometimes taking it away to cool. Then the inspection, the decision to pass her thumbs through. And they of the house watching her, and the children sent away to play. Sent to the garden perhaps, place where they were allowed once in a twelvemonth. And she who was to have the new child would be creaking the floor-boards upstairs. For they had sent her up there just in case. For this old woman had the evil eye and there was no knowing what spell she might cast on the harmless one before it came into the world.

And down in the kitchen they would be watching her. Smiling at her and reaching her a chair to stand on, and a hammer when the time came for her to raise her thin, long arms to nail the telltale charm over the back door. Reaching her coat and giving her the payment and letting her stay, if she asked, for the extra warm. The maid sent with a message to keep the children longer in the garden. And to keep *her* upstairs, her especially safe up there.

The old woman safely gone and the children in from the garden asking about the black bone on the long string. Warned not to touch it for it was half a thing of Satan. And she who had come downstairs was told not to worry, for in the morning she would know.

St. Asaph is a small city. With a cathedral and a see dating from the sixth century. The cathedral is a big village church almost, and coming upon it I had to pause to remember that here indeed reigned a bishop.

The first cathedral was burned in 1282. And Glyndwr, ever in argument with the English, destroyed some of the new building. It was rebuilt again in 1480 but not finally finished until 1770. And in the years between not left always to the chants and slow solemn communion, for in the Civil Wars this cathedral was used as a stable.

St. Asaph now dreamy and lovely with all the peace of a cathedral city. No bustling stores or super chromium service. The cathedral tempers all, and Ecclesiasticus reigns in the city.

Up the valley towards the sea, and three miles from the coast I came to Rhuddlan with its castle famous in Welsh history. Here where the Statute was drawn up with its laws for Wales. And on the Marsh of Rhuddlan was fought a sad, unhappy battle for the Welsh against Offa in earlier days. Offa of Mercia who beat Caradoc in this battle, and with bitterness lingering on when the fight was over. So that Offa's men killed all prisoners and it is said that those of the Welsh who escaped across the marsh were all cut off by the tide and drowned. Sad is the tune, *Marsh of Rhuddlan*, in memory to the Welshmen who died here. But the motor coaches, green and blue and golden lettered, from the English cities shine on the road to the sea. Hardly a look at the old, tired, ruined castle. For it's only a few minutes to the sea and the sands, and Punch and Judy are happy and nothing sad must come to a holiday.

I am at the sea again, the sea of the north of Wales. And there is a difference here. For there is none of the wildness and loneliness of the west coast. The sea here is civilised and respectable. Here are ships passing with blue, lazy smoke, half of sky, half of water. The roads are busy and are edged with ordered chalets and coloured villas. The roads have cat's-eye indicators let in the pavement edges for the night motorist, and there are white lines and safe islands and macadam safely cambered.

And sighting the sea between rust sand and the coarse grass of the dunes there is colour, always in the summer. Bobbing tight-skinned heads of women, cap-helmeted and chin-strapped to keep dry the soft hair for the dance to-night. The gayness of many bathing costumes; wraps flapping and beating in the breeze of the sea. Children ride painted ducks. Or wait impatient as more air is pumped in to make stiff and safe the floating toy.

Young men run giggling girls across the sands and old women lie back in the first surf and kick legs to the sky.

And a man sells balloons. Tight and almost bursting and all making a hum and a ring as they rub one against the other high on the strings above his head. He walks the sands shouting, and letting the wind from the sea carry his voice to every group of mothered children. He has walked from the town up the coast and will go on right around the Point. And only stopping when his hands are quite empty or the last children have been taken home to bed.

I shall go the coast way later. But now my way will be to the east into Flintshire. To the towns between the Vale of Clwyd and the edge of the sands of the Dee.

Flintshire is a tiny county of low hills and gentle plain. Famous once for butter and cheese and honey. And from the old straw beehives the metheglin was made and drunk. And from the hills came millstones and Caergwrle had "a spring as clear as crystal, and yet it will turn whitish with oil of tartar; it also turns green with syrup of violets, and red with logwood. A gallon will yield 220 grains of sediment of which 56 are earth, and 154 are sea-salt and limestone. It appears to be impregnated with a calcarious nitre and sea-salt and if drunk to a quart or two will purge pretty well. It has cured a woman that had a loathsome scurf all over her body, by drinking three pints of this water a day."

I go to Holywell, famous for its holy spring of such strength that in flowing away it worked one corn mill, six copper and brass mills and four cotton mills.

The spring of the well was disturbed but the holy well still is in being. Still to it come the sick. The bathchair and the crutch thrown away. A last pull at the wheels and the creaking chair is sold second-hand or left as a witness. This well of St. Winifred. She a fair virtuous girl who would not yield to Prince Caradoc. He, very annoyed, cut off her head, and where it fell a sudden fast spring came, clear and cold, never hot, never freezing.

But Winifred did not die, for her uncle, St. Beuno, came out of a church nearby. Came quickly and joined the head back to the body with earnest prayer. She lived again and Caradoc fell dead, his body black and his soul taken away at once by evil spirits to everlasting torment. The girl became an abbess and is now sanctified.

The well originally gave water at the rate of about twenty-four tons a minute. But in mining operations the well source has been tapped and the water is now pumped to the well.

Protestants smile. The chapel people prefer torment in this world as a sure guide for salvation in the next. Remember that in 1784 "harping and dancing were decreasing in Wales, by the introduction of the Methodists who overrun the country". And now prayer is offered for the heathen souls of the Catholic. For crutch and bathchair were sent to make Jobs of all and there is no arguing with the Almighty.

I go on to Flint and to Shotton. Flint where Richard II was handed over prisoner to the Duke of Lancaster. The town has now a great rayon works, bringing much prosperity to the town. In the last century the place had a "ragged and repulsive aspect". A castle secure once on a rock of freestone close to the Dee. The course of the estuary river changes with the centuries. And sand

and mud never gleam with new-left salt wetness. Grasses come, the marsh grows. Old mooring rings rust, never the smooth run of rope. The polish of hemp slipping with the swaying ship, gone for ever. Only now rush and bogwort and sweet meadow grasses. The rings taken away. The iron melted or the rings used to tie cattle in new-made cowshed or as a halter tie in some ammonia-sweet stable.

Shotton with its works and red the night sky with industrial, perpetual sunset.

And to Mold where Richard Wilson, the painter, is buried. Mold lies over the Clwydian Hills from the Vale of Clwyd. This is the county town of Flintshire and a place where many roads meet, a red spider's web on the map. Roads go out to Wrexham and to Flint and to Rhyl, to Ruthin and to Chester.

And I go over to the Vale of Clwyd again, up the valley and to the edge of Liverpool Bay. I leave behind the mines and the busy towns. The ugly trellis with the lonely, high, spinning wheel. And at the bottom the black heap of sheds, the mountain of coal waste. The mines of East Denbighshire with their loud-tongued, generous-hearted miners. The old marks of coal, black on the face where once the diamond fell and cut. Arms with the black pores and eyes that blink in strong summer sunlight. Fond of spending and often the piano in the house which none of the family can play. But the pound note is always ready for next door if they need it. And with hard times come a puzzled enmity at the hard hearts of the fortunate ones who ride in cars and have saved with the years.

I go up the valley knowing that the rest of my journey will see no pattern of factory chimneys raising black smoke to a fair sky. I am away from the smudge, now. Away from the industry of the north-east corner, away from East Denbighshire. Away from where the factory imp has wiped his hands. And left the chimneys and the skylighted roofs and the rows of narrow cottages, grey peas in the iron pod. With back doors into little yards, and the little yards with lavatories and the washhouses side by side. In the front windows the geranium pots for defiance, and sometimes the red pots wrapped round with a length of crêpe paper, green or yellow. With all the spring gone out of the paper with the sunlight and the whole sagging and water-stained from the weekly watering with the old teapot.

The lead mines have been worked, and now it is the coal. And when the one pit has all gone, the seam filled with water, then all is abandoned. And dreadful shells of buildings stand up in memorial. With slates blowing off one at a time and the rafters left in bare straight even lines. Mortar loosening from the walls with every fierce day of rain and sharp night of frost. Window-panes knocked jagged by small straight-aiming boys, and the high boiler chimney with the green weeds and the tall grass on top of it, higher than the old bent finger of the lightning-conductor. Birds fly in and out and perch on rusted wheels, sparrows play in the stoking pit. And great derisive crows cackle in and cackle out with a flap of wings. The deep shafts fill with the water of the years, black and deep and with pretty green scum wobbling when a stone is dropped with a far-sounding splash. Around the shafts the farmers have built barbed-wire fences and councils have put up leaning notices of *Danger*. And only the brambles grow happy and well watered where once men rose and fell in wide wooden buckets, and wheels turned and new engines hissed. Engines kept clean and bright by proud enginemen and sweating boilermen.

The ruins remain with none of the old beauty of abbeys serene and oriel windowed. But crumble in an ugly way from year to year. Old factories, old mines. Not like the abbeys in well-watered meadows and with the view of the sheep hills. Or the castles face to the sea and back to the mountains. But in a wasteland, all the good sweet land ruined by old, tippled, poisoned earth. The bramble grows and a gayness comes only with the dandelions and the acres of the foxgloves. Dandelions yellow to fade to rounded heads of tell-the-time. Red foxgloves to wither and the brown seeds to spread in their thousands to make gaudy the patch next summer.

Children play and sheep nibble. And sometimes the horse of a local coal merchant, some Jane or Bess, searches each Sunday and each night for the short grass.

Balls bounce and the boys sling the bat always away from the pit. But sometimes the ball rolls and slips under the wire fence. Floats with the scum and last year's fallen leaves. The boys watch it float, uneasy to lean over and with bat in hand a hope to tap it to the side. Sometimes father comes with a long garden rake to strain and reach. But always a first testing of the edge of the pit, the earth side of the shaft. For here is the hundred feet of water. Far more dangerous than any rolling sea or clear-watered lake.

Sometimes there is a game of Red Indians in the ruins. Sending all crows and sparrows away, refugees from make-believe. The game over, and the last shout as home to bed. Making the happy sounds for the distant listener, of children playing in the last heat of a July day.

Along the painted line, now. Prestatyn to Llandudno. A line bulging out sometimes into beautiful beads, enamel and gay for the summer. Grey, sea-splashed in the winter.

The lamp-posts are bright, the baskets full of flowers and dainty with moss and fragile fern. Watered by the man on the ladder, tip of a spout and all's well for three days. Preserve through the summer and unhook for the steamy glass-house in the winter.

The promenades are stormy, the piers are sturdy. Concert parties with the star names and bands sweet and bands nasty. Bathing beauties splashing and girls with dainty bottles tan so quick. Toes in the sea or a deck-chair for threepence. The streets are clean and the houses painted. No lonely walk for the cigarettes. The chip shops are white and chromium, the smell regulated.

I stand on a footbridge at Prestatyn, a high steelwork bridge, severe and straight over the railway. A bridge square-ended with no arch of grace; no wet cold stone. A bridge over the railway, many-lined and hazy with heat when the July sun shines. Straight-set rails which clang and echo when the coming train is only a shaking dot in the distance.

This is the way the Irish Mail comes, with the white boards on the sides of the carriage roofs and the name blurring by in a long black smear. Craning over and I can see in through the windows. The book in hands and the grey-white as a newspaper is turned. And a stiffer, greater whiteness as the dining-cars rock smoothly by.

Where the Irish Mail now rattles the railway by the sea once went another road of romance.

The Romans made great roads across North and South Wales. And three joining roads up through the middle of the country. Straight and level, made by the many aching backs, walked by the marching feet. This road along the North Wales coast along which Paulinus took his Roman legions to the last kill of the Druids across the Menai Strait. And where Harold, last Saxon king, rode in the years before Hastings. A highway by the sea. And out to sea the memory of all the blue days. Ships small, and great-funnelled liners trailing gentle smoke for Liverpool. Once the great white ships in from the Indies and the Americas, Africa and the distant East. Slaves black and the shackles bolted safe to wooden walls. In to Liverpool to the slave cellars. Out again, slow where the planes now fast fly, out to the great white houses of Virginia, lawns and trees and the shaded drives.

Ships across Liverpool Bay bringing in silks and the strange, sweet-smelling spices, ivory and rare ebony.

The slaves and the spices gone with the great white ships. Only now the puffing funnels bringing in the dried fruit and the food refrigerated and dehydrated.

I have stayed often in Prestatyn. A town clean and bright as if fresh from a perpetual wash. The railway through the centre, a kind of line dividing the bourgeois, up on the heights live the well-to-do. The other houses are flat by the sea and where the creeping mists of the night come. And out to sea the bell-buoy clangs. Warning that here a proud ship ran on the sands. With the winds and the tides to tear her to pieces over the winter months.

A good road to Rhyl. The town is, like Prestatyn, in Flintshire. Coast towns with the beaches flat and smooth. Like great ant-hills levelled out. The bathers thousand trotting to the sea, lying on the beaches. Evening comes and they go to the life of the town. Tide comes and only a last boy and girl walk, bare feet on the white first edge of the waves. To-morrow back to Birmingham or Blackburn. Last walk on the firm sand, last kicks at the shells. You'll write, won't you? Promise faithfully?

And looking out to sea all the world is rose, and trams and pounding tools and houses neat in rows are away in the dark, a world that never was, never dare be.

From the town comes a distant music. Coming louder as the night sea breeze slackens. Then lost again with this breeze fresh from the flat of the sea. The lights of the towns twinkle behind, red and green, and greater yellow stains in the sky.

Abergele was once three miles from the sea, but the sea is the constant enemy now. The last enemy who pushes the sand, breaks through. Sweeps away neat concrete and twists iron bars. The fight is on, the watch must ever be kept.

Old Colwyn, Colwyn Bay and Rhos-on-Sea join now, their last houses straggling out one into the other. Villages once but catering now for every taste in Colwyn Bay. And what village could do that?

Llandudno developed as a watering-place from about the middle of the last century. And now who has not seen the adverts? The Great Orme is a headland out to sea with views far and green over the Irish Sea. High to over seven hundred feet this rocky cliff and once said to be an island. And on the western side there was once an abbey, Gogarth Abbey. Monks cowled and sober and chants by the sea. Now the bathing cap and the flirting laugh, boogie-woogie, honky-tonk and twelve-bar blues.

The last of my three vales now, Conway Valley. And almost a more lovely land than Llangollen or the Vale of Clwyd.

An old famous river, the Conway. Noted now for its salmon, silver dainties and fished strict to season and to licence. Haunted by water bailiffs and dark nights, poachers and Game Laws known better than the Bible. The net across the river, the bottom weighted and on top the bobbing, floating corks. At each side of the river men, waist-high in water, walk the river bed, swim through the deep pools. And all the time the net is swept on, and every now and again hauled in to the one bank for the catch to be taken out and put in a sack. Though modern poaching is a much more scientific business and dynamite used, shocking and dreadful, in some of the Welsh rivers. And handfuls of lime and spearing and other tricks well known to gamekeepers and bailiffs and disgusting to their Worships, white-haired and sedate and a cut of salmon a seven o'clock joy in the evening.

The Conway was well known once for its pearl fisheries. The Romans are said to have conquered Wales especially to have control of these. Julius Cæsar sent a specially decorated breastplate of British pearls back to Rome. And Catherine, wife of Charles II, had a lustrous beauty given her by Welshman Richard Wynn.

I start at Conway town. Conway with its castle on the edge of the sea, this most wonderful castle of the thirteenth century where Edward I and Eleanor spent a Christmas Court and where Eleanor grew the first sweet-peas in the garden over the river.

This castle in the angle between the sea and the river and moated on its landward side. With walls fifteen foot thick and vaults for food and dungeons for prisoners. And a tower for the king and a tower for the queen. The Great Hall is roofless now, one of the Earls of Conway furnishing his Irish estates from the fittings soon after the Restoration.

A merry Christmas Court is must have been, safe against the sea and with the moat and the river to keep away the uneasy Welsh.

Now the railway thunders by, fast with the mails to Ireland. And on Bank Holidays the coast road is a jam-pot of flies with motorists; yellow motor coaches for crawling wasps. All in a great hurry, for a holiday is to be measured in miles and sweet-peas are things for flower shows and Christmas is only one day, anyway.

On through the towns of the Conway Valley. Llanrwst, famous for its harps and Bettws-y-Coed, now an exhibition beauty spot. Capel Curig with its lakes and a starting-point for the many climbs up to Snowdon. And the famous Nant Francon Pass, with mountains up like walls from the damp, boggy bottom and the whole giving a feeling of a great trap, jaws open and at any moment ready for the sudden snap, and end to everything.

Llanrwst was once famous for its harp-makers. David Cae Ceiliog was one of these. He who lived in the local almshouse, but who would never quite finish his instruments in there for fear that the chatter of the old women of the place should spoil the tune of his harp. This man used to fetch the materials for his harp-making from Chester and he would walk the journey pushing a wheel-barrow with the bought necessities for his work. By apprenticeship this David had been a shipbuilder. Another Llanrwst harp-maker was Rowland Griffith. The harps of these makers sold for about eight pounds in the eighteenth century.

Up to the beginning of the fifteenth century hair was used for harp stringing and it was only at that time that gut was first used.

And up to the end of that century only a single row of strings was used; the flats and sharps were made by a cunning trick of finger and thumb.

Another old Welsh instrument was the crwth. This had six strings and four of these were played with a bow. The remaining two strings were plucked with the thumb as a bass accompaniment. A sweet-toned instrument, a mellow tenor. The bridge was curved down through the air hole and was fixed to the inside of the back.

The last great crwth player was Rhys Crythor of Elizabethan days.

Sweet harps and their playing was once a delight in Welsh inns and homes of the gentry. It was the owner of Euloe Castle, near Northop by Chester, who used to give a badge of a silver harp for the sweetest harpist in Wales.

Sometimes on my way I have seen the small house in a corner of a wet field. A pasture of cowslips and summer buttercups which yellow the boot with pollen after a minute's walk. A field which has been brought into use by piping and draining. Long trenches made and the brown lengths of baked clay, four-inch piping laid carefully, a great fan out from the little brook which runs gurgle and trickle, moss-sided and fern-shaded at the side of the field. Trenches which are filled in and over the years the clay pipes below drain the field, carry all the water from the many little springs direct to the brook.

The old drains were made of flat stones. On either side and roofed. A tunnel made to make the land a pasture, to take away the squelch, the pull at the foot after winter rain.

And set in a corner of this field is a house. Set in this wasteland, ground kept fertile only by constant care. A perpetual trapping for moles who, in making their own tunnels, disturb and clog the carefully-laid pipes.

Moles are caught with traps. Either a two-pronged affair carefully set in the tunnel of the mole and which it sets off by the pressure of its own body. Or a tiny wooden barrel, open at both ends, laid flush in the run and a great strangling wire worked by a spring to squeeze the life out of the blue-black body. Or perhaps poison is laid, earthworms dipped in strychnine. But here the body is lost and mole skins sell well. The animal is skinned with a sharp pocket-knife and the skin is nailed to a board in a toolshed. Stretched out with a nail in each corner. Left to dry and then sold. Sometimes the skins are kept and then sent away for a mole-skin waistcoat to be made, winter-warm and hard-wearing.

But this house, set in the lonely field? Perhaps this is a Hafod-un-nos, a clod house? These were once built in Wales. A scheme for the obtaining of land free by quick house-building.

A corner of waste ground was chosen in the parish and then the builder made his plans. His friends all came to help him to build this house of one night. For if they succeeded in raising a house and having smoke from the chimney with the sunrise then the land on which the house was built became the builder's property.

The walls of the houses were usually made of turf. The roof was a prefabricated affair. Generally the latter was thatched with straw or rushes. But for the scheme to succeed it was essential that there should be smoke from the chimney with the rising sun.

But the new landowner had claim to more land than that on which his house was actually built. He could claim more by the throwing of an axe.

The owner stood by his door and threw an axe in all directions. And the distance he could throw was the boundary of the land which he could claim as his.

A thrill and an excitement there must have been as the new fire was laid and there was a race for the smoke to come.

The house has been rebuilt now, more solid, stone walled and slated. In the house now lives, perhaps, a roadman. Or the old widow, black dressed, and who rolls each day the crumbs into bread rolls for the tits and the finches. And who has a white proud cat who sleeps all day snug in the red-curtained window. An old lady who lost her husband on a May night. He who had the mistress. The fair-haired maid from the Hall who had all domination over the jobbing gardener, he who could plant and transplant and scorned all glass with the cunning of his hands. He and the girl used the same fork of the full-blossomed apple tree, the two ends of the same rope. And after they'd cut her down her hair, they said, had been full of pink and white apple blossom.

People say that he has come back again and sleeps in the white cat of the window. And that the girl runs the countryside at May-time, with look and call into every high apple tree.

Every parish has its ghosts. In a land of invasion and struggle and cruel reprisal all the tormented spirits are supposed to linger. Prisoners tortured and the lust for revenge over every racial wrong. The Border country particularly is seeped in the hatred and deep in the quiet soil all the old fighters must lie buried; far below the turning plough and the digging garden spade. All the old bones of the invaders aching to march into this strange mountain land of the west. Where the dark-haired, strange-tongued people lived. The redness is gone to goodly greenness and only on a wild night can the ghosts walk. When a high wind blows clouds before the moon and makes fast black shadows on the roads. And when the cock pheasants are uneasy and a farm dog cries to the hunter's moon. Across the valley the farmhouse lights go out, one by one. Only a late car sweeps the sky with its flashing lights.

Farmer sleeps and in the cowhouses the cattle rattle the chains with a sleepy draw at the hay. In the village the policeman walks up the street, from black-shadowed houses to the moonlight alleys between the rows. Stopping on the bridge with a half-look to the black water and the moonraking clouds reflected. The policeman the last to bed and only a thought for the petty sessions or a half-remembered sheep-dipping. So to bed, policeman, and all the valley sleeps. The dog turns in the old kennel and with a last whine puts nose on paw. And the pheasants are quiet now that some vibrating noise has gone. Give a last cackle and the woods have only the break of twigs, the night noises.

Then all the old Welsh ghosts come out. Owain Glyndwr to walk the hills. To find the castles he took, still standing; the churches he burned, built again. To find the Welsh and the English mixing in the towns, neighbours, and with no drawn knife. With Welsh spoken and the hills still gentle, the shape of the mountains grand against the blue night sky.

Caradoc walking again and finding his old enemies the Romans gone, and their language academic and spoken awkwardly by scholars and apothecaries.

The Welsh princes and the bards and the saintly hermits slipping out in the moonlight hours to see the old places. Recall wasted life and wasted effort. Crawl back again when the first dawn comes over the hated eastern plain. England is waking and the old Welsh must away. But the days of blood struggle are over. And though there are those who would see Wales free, the last Englishman hanged on the Border, yet perhaps the world's too small just now for roots so deep.

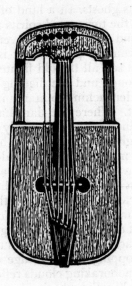

IV. THE LAST LONELINESS

THE LAST LONELINESS

To the lonely places, the remote country. Where live the pure Welsh and the half-breeds of the Border are another race, almost. To places now where the children play Welsh in the school yards, with call and chatter and noisy shout. Where live white-locked old men who have never been into England, and slow-knitting old women who think that a double-decker bus is a journey to the brothel. Here live people who have watched sea, watched mountain. People who never make a journey further than the weekly trip to market and who wear clothes old into the years.

People here, too, who hate the English.

And there are many in these quiet places who have never used a telephone, never known the frightening whiteness of the dentist, never known a bathroom except the laying of the hip-bath by the kitchen fire on the Saturday night.

Men who read only the Bible and the days-old news in some weekly paper. Women who do not know the silkiness of an electric iron and who cook on iron ranges, black roaring furnaces.

The last loneliness. The county island of Anglesey; the mountains and the heather cliffs of Caernarvonshire. Places where there is much quietness, height of mountain and wave of unsailed sea-water.

Green Anglesey with its farms, and shores north to the busy sea; island which the sea lanes curve round as the ships come in to Liverpool. Island where the Druids last lived and where they made the human sacrifice. Anglesey with Holyhead town, packet station for Ireland.

Caernarvonshire the county with the jaw into the sea. A land's-end with the afterthought of Bardsey three miles out, the fast tides for a racing bridge. The county with the high crowning glory of Snowdon and with the Pilgrim Way of the Lleyn Peninsula. High mountains and the coasts of worn sullen rocks and tempting untrod sand. County with the city of Bangor, respectable with its cathedral, gay with its university. With the town of Caernarvon and its three-acre castle, linked to the English Crown with its association of the Princes of Wales. The county with lovely Bettws-y-Coed with its Swallow Falls, and with Aberdaron and its famous Dick, master of many languages. Of castled Conway and harboured Pwllheli. Llanberis and the naked mountains and the train puffing right to the top of the high advertised Snowdon, a constant fly on the old tolerant monster.

My last way is through this loneliness. This far-away part of Wales which was the last desire of all invaders and where independence struggled on. A way through a country of mountain and cliff and sea. With view and climb and annoyed, rock-beating water. Heather and peeps to sea and the enticement of Snowdonia. A way, too, to two islands.

Anglesey, winter-misted with the moan of ships. A coast with the story of wrecks and salvage for those who waved good ships on. An island of summer loveliness, white-grey houses on the slow-rolling hills.

And the other island, Bardsey. This the sacred place and the end of the Pilgrim Way which went along the Lleyn Peninsula. A little island where many saints are buried and where in the middle of the last century human bones were so plentiful that they were used as fences.

I go back to Conway and from there my way will be along the Caernarvonshire coast to Bangor. The gayer North Wales resorts left behind now. From Conway on to Penmaenmawr with its headland out to sea and with the railway and the road hugging anxiously the bottom of it. This road was built in 1772 to replace the old steep way, high and dangerous over the top of the rock. The old road, the Pass of Penmaenmawr, famous for its disasters and a constant worry.

Here the coach travellers shivered and record the agony of the watch of the drop to the sea. Write of the steepness of the road and of the little protection between the way and the precipice.

At either end of the Pass there was once an inn where travellers could fortify themselves against the ordeal. And if surviving, then the drink in thankfulness. The tankard to still the quivering stomach.

Safe on the good road I go to Llanfairfechan. It is evening and the promise of a good to-morrow comes red out of the west. To the right is the island coast of Anglesey and the smooth blueness of Puffin Island. The town of Beaumaris far away across the mouth of the Strait on the Anglesey side. The town low lying and shapeless in the distance, with a patchwork of brown and green fields, and sometimes the white of a whitewashed house. All fast losing colour and passing deep into shadow against the ebbing sky.

Can I forget you? Or will my heart remind me, how once we lived . . .

From the house the radio plays and I stand by the sea and listen. Then a draw of curtains and the yellow light turns red and blue and far away through the chintz. The music stops. The sea is heard again, the roll of the tide up the Menai Strait. Duck fly flailing-winged for the distant marsh and over on Anglesey the lighthouse licks light. Puffin Island and the end of Anglesey join in the darkness.

Llanfairfechan, unspoiled stone-built town backed by the mountains and with Puffin Island the view across the sea, that and the low coastline of Anglesey. No straight horizon of sea here, with the trailing smoke of steamers. But a land to watch, and the lighthouse at night. The fast narrow seas are a laughing noisy barrier when the tide comes galloping up the Menai Strait, to surge and fill and hide the sand with foam-edged water.

On the one side the sea and on the other the mountains. High mountains of Caernarvonshire. And from the mountains come down the farmers and their wives, sometimes, on a summer evening to the side of the sea. Come down to Llanfairfechan in the car when the harvest is in, and the children want to play by the sea which they can see blue and ever so near from the top attic windows of the farmhouse. And so they are brought down and now that they are near the sea they are a little frightened. The noise as the tide comes up, and there are all the other children to share the secret.

The parents sit in the car or awkward on the sand in suit and staid costume. Shy of the strangers who come and show body, and live for the feel of the water, the heat of the sun. These farmers who strip only when the body sweats, and then there still is the flannel shirt, the vest and the dark trousers. They who wear the woollen socks and the great black boots, no dainty sandals.

And driving home to the farm in the evening, back to the mountains, there is the uneasiness. And a hope that now the children will be satisfied. To-morrow it must be work again with no sand to trickle through bare toes and the distant sea only a thing to be watched for the turn of the weather.

The mountain farmers ih Caernarvonshire, Merionethshire,

upper Montgomeryshire and Denbighshire, how do they earn a living? How easy is it to gain money from this land of the wonderful view and the stony ground, the blaze of gorse and the thin-bladed grass, the smokeless air and the blue-rocked estate?

Pounds, shillings and the pence are gained from the sale of the wool and from the sale of the lambs for Welsh mutton. A few calves are reared, the heifer calves kept to raise stock cows, and the bull calves reared to bullocks, fattened and sold. Butter is made from the milk and a few eggs are sold from the hens running loose around the house. At Christmas time geese and ducks are reared and sold at the Christmas markets.

Christmas with its carol singing and plum puddings and the whole spirit of December, white or green. In the cities the stores have the bright lights and the darting children. Windows with crêpe and silent Father Christmas, stiff as scarecrows and brought up from the basement storeroom to stuff a window with Christmas. And the children peep from behind curtains to watch the postmen with van or truck.

What of Christmas in the mountains and the valleys, what of the Welsh Christmas? The mountains of North Wales where grow little fir Christmas trees all the year round, straight rows planted. And to this country where the snow comes soon, lasts the longest. And the valleys, where there are no great shops hawking Christmas. And the coast towns lonely when all the visitors have gone, Christmas a place for home. Who would spend Christmas by the sea, in camp or lodging-house? What of the lonely farms and villages where the post comes at nine always, and always goes at four in the afternoon?

North Wales has a good Christmas, not so much, perhaps, tinsel and crêpe bells, but rather an atmosphere of good feeling. A good material time, what with all the firs to be sent away in lorries, and the red-berried green holly to be cut and sold at so much a hundredweight. Mistletoe, too, not now the sacred Druid bough, but sold in bunches to the produce merchants. This parasite, cultivated and unpruned to keep romance alive, to sell at Christmas time.

And on mountain and valley farm there is the selling of geese, of turkeys, and ducks, and fat chickens. All reared from young stock and tended and well fed through the autumn days, carefully and tenderly. All the short days of the year the young turkeys are kept out of the wet, out of the rain, for the damp will do them harm. And with bacon and eggs in plenty and bread and milk always as the main breakfast meal, the bought breakfast oats and cereals are made into mash with separated milk to raise fat ducks, great waddling plump geese.

The fowl are sold either dead or dressed. If dead, then white in their feathers, or turkey blue-black. Dressed, they are feathered on the farms, a whole night of this with all the neighbours helping together. The fowl are cleaned and made tempting and tasty with sprigs of parsley, green and fresh. And they are sold in either the dead or the alive Christmas markets. The alive is a fortnight before Christmas and the ducks and the geese and the turkeys are brought in alive with tape-tied legs. Tape of coloured cloth made from some old suit and cut up. Brought in baskets and laid in rows in the market halls of the market towns; and there the dealers come to buy.

Or taken to the dead market, where the fowl are brought in feathered and dressed and tempting Christmas dinners laid out on greaseproof paper, long rows of the appetising dead. With the farmers' wives standing in their black cloth behind the benches, anxious, watching tombstones. Dealers come in their own overalls with assistants and ready money.

Time was when the Christmas markets were slow, when the poulterers' shops even in the country towns had the rows of imported birds hanging unhappy on steel hooks. And the farmers brought in their fowls to the live market only and never a risk for the dead market. For if the ducks were not sold they could be taken home again. Reprieved with an unhappy loosening of the tying tape. Allowed to walk away and a hope that their living would be justified by the egg-laying. Big, wonderful, rich duck eggs to make the yellow custard for the dinner.

On Christmas Day, perhaps, there is a concert in the village hall, some distant party of singers and reciters and penillion singers coming. Or there may be a drama company to give a Welsh play, with the stock plots and the superficial themes. The deacon who marries again and the spinster on the Sunday School trip. The farm lads sit around the Hall, perched like sparrows on the windowsills, big black-booted feet dangling. The J.P.s of the village and the deacons sit on the front rows of chairs, with seats numbered. At the back half of the Hall are the benches, backless, and often in the darkness a farm girl is hauled backwards. A kicking and a shouting and the police comes in with his bamboo walking stick with its well-known hard knob.

Carol parties sometimes go round. Well trained and well organised but having a habit of singing Welsh hymns in the minor key and seldom happy carols. Hymns with the memory of some bleak funeral giving a plaintiveness to the singing. These parties come often in the middle of the night. And my Christmas visitors wake suddenly to this music and it is hard to explain to them that we enjoy this sad singing.

Santa Claus comes to long, black, borrowed, woollen stockings held up to the bedposts by a great wad of binder twine. This cord which last summer was used to fasten the sheaves of wheat and which was cut free at threshing time. The presents bought in the market town are smuggled to the house under the old paper crumpled at the bottom of the empty butter basket. The horse and trap, or the car, has to be the sledge and reindeer. And jingle bells the way the loose white gate on the mountain road swings in the wind, the worn latch clinking in, clinking out.

I go along the coast road from Llanfairfechan on to Aber, tiny and facing the great flat of the Lavin Sands. These smooth and dry when the tide is out and a tempting place to walk to Anglesey. But the sand dips and hollows the water by the island coast, and it is a race back to the green field safety of Aber shore. There are waterfalls at Aber, waters rushing anxious for the narrow beauty of the Strait.

Near Aber, Llewelyn ap Iorweth had his palace. And after the siege of Montgomery Castle he brought William de Breos here as a prisoner. The wife of Llewelyn was Joan, a daughter of John, King of England.

William de Breos was a handsome, cultivated man and gained the affection of Llewelyn and the love of his wife. Joan became his mistress and the love affair went on until de Breos was ransomed. And it was not until the baron had left that Llewelyn discovered the secret. For revenge he invited de Breos to visit him again to renew their friendship. The baron came, was immediately hung on a hill opposite the palace. Tradition says that the next morning the palace bard went to the unsuspecting Joan and asked her what she would give to see William. She answered that she would give Wales and England and Llewelyn to see her William. They then took her out and showed her her lover hanging from the tree on the hill.

And from Aber I go along the coast to Bangor. The road between the mountains and the sea of the Menai Strait. With Anglesey, green and brown across the water. And in the left distance the mountains. Blue in summer and with the winter tinged with the first and the last of the snows.

In autumn the summer blueness of the mountains becomes ridged and streaked with whiteness. A first morning when in the valley the cowman and the postman look up, with a tightening of jackets, a fastening of buttons.

Snow coming to the high ground and then going again, off and on the whole of the winter. And one day in spring when the sun makes spidery shadows of the trees, the streaks of snow left from the winter blizzards, fade. Become less every day in the sunshine and run down to the valleys in the clear, cold water of the brooks. Rush and tinkle over brown stones; surge against the boulders.

A winter of much snow means much loss in the mountains, worry and labour for the farmers. A hurry to protect young stock and the older animals having to be fed on the moors and mountainside. Ice to be broken at the watering places. But to the valley farmer the snow is hardly a disaster what with stock always within easy reach of the farmhouse and good shelter.

To the hill farmer the snow means worry. For his main stock are the sheep scattered in their thousands over the mountains; sheep walks of a thousand acres, far away and a pony ride from the house.

Welsh mountain sheep are hardy, and able to live for some time even if buried under the snow, making a warmth for themselves. And so there must be days of digging under every shelf of rock and under the stone walls where the sheep may have crouched for shelter. A digging with great wide farmyard shovels, scraping the drifts of white, formless snow away. Trenches dug with the hope for life at the bottom. A hold of the fleece and the sheep lifted up and left to sag again, with a look for the straightening knee, the lift of head. Gin and brandy and the live sheep are carried away to some corner of the walls where they can be watched together. And be fed with glucose and covered with old meal sacks, a grey huddle together for warmth.

The shepherd who walks the hills in the places where the mountain pony cannot reach, and where the way is too steep for the bicycle. He who goes with a stout walking stick, a thing cut from the lowland hedge and carved into shape in the autumn evenings.

A hobby of some farmers and farm labourers, this cutting and making of walking sticks. Not made for the selling, but for the pleasure of making only. Or in competition for the arts and crafts section of some local Eisteddfod.

Walking the roads sided with high hedges, a watch for the straight hazel stick, the ash with a thick base. A look through the thick of the thorn hedge in colour to the straight pieces of wood there. The blackthorn stick which will have a hardness, a toughness.

The sticks are cut from the hedge and always a good length of spare wood is left. And a piece of the thick root, too, is cut out if possible. For if this curves, or is thick, it can be made into an easy handle.

The stick is cut and hung up in the outhouse of the farm buildings. Hung there among the bushing-hooks and the scythes and the old broken blades of the hay-mower.

Left there for a long time to dry and the sap to half wither away. Then some wet day comes and the steaming is done. A kettle is set on the red kitchen fire and comes a watch until the steam spouts steady.

Then the stick is straightened in the steam. A careful bending to take away the curves and the wobbles. The stick is quickly straightened and set in between boards and screwed in a vice.

After a time it is taken out and then come the hours of work with a penknife. A job for the evenings, the length of the stick between the knees and the point of it set carefully on an opened-out sheet of newspaper to catch all the little chippings, the curl of the peelings. The head of the stick is carved into some fancy design. A dog's wild head or the end of the curved handle trimmed into some flower bud.

Comes a smoothing with a piece of old window glass, the one

cut side as a kind of scraper file. And after that a last loving polish with sandpaper.

Varnish and bright ferrule and the stick is ready for the market-day journey. And it is only with the years and when another stick has been made that this one will be used for the everyday walking of the mountain.

In the dark little hall of the house there is a wide old drain-pipe set on end. Some spare pipe from a time of draining taken and stained and finished to the imitation brown of oak. This is set up in the hall corner and used as the stand for the walking sticks. All the new bright ends standing here and a rattle and shake when the pipe has to be moved at the annual spring-cleaning.

And in the same dark hallway there will be the two wooden pegs fast to the wall, and there the blue, double-barrelled shot-gun. Most of the upland farmers are good shots, poaching game from their own land. But with little regard for the genteel side of the game. Season and sitting target ignored and a covey of part-

ridge on the white cold snow under a wide oak tree a temptation never ignored.

The old local poacher I once knew who talked always in Welsh to his dog. A strange, one-eared dog, and said to have been something of a sheep-killer until the lamb watchers had shot away his ear with a near-miss in the moonlight.

He had this dog and the old gun as well. A thing which was deserving of a glass case, a description and a printing in a catalogue. For it was a muzzle-loader, dangerous, but a sure killing when old Davie raised it to his rheumaticky shoulder.

He loaded it from the pouches and canisters he had rattling from the old brass belt around the middle of him. A belt made of rings interlocked with one another and at the very back a little leather purse which he unlocked with a finely-wrought iron key.

And at the front of the belt dangled the leather pouch of lead shot and the tin canister of gunpowder. There to his belt; and over his back the ramrod fastened by a stout piece of whipcord.

Old Davie would set the gun against a gate to load it. Setting it so that the muzzle pointed far away to the grey of the sky. And there loading his gun carefully with the gunpowder and the pellets and ramming down the charge carefully with his ramrod.

But he had the accident. And that no fault of his. It was that his ramrod got tight in the barrel and he could not free it. And in desperation Davie fired the charge. He never found his ramrod and now his gun is quite useless. For try as he will in all the gun-smiths they only smile at him and shake their shop heads. And they want to sell him the fancy pair of guns snug in a felt case.

Davie uses snares now and works his ferrets twice as hard. And always as he digs he hopes that he will find his ramrod again, rusty but still a thing to load his "muzzle-loader".

The old poacher with his felt waistcoat, a pincushion of fish hooks as he lifts up his jacket to reach his purse at the back of him. He who once poached out of hunger. But now his pension a whole wealth to him in his way of living. Openly now he meets the pro-duce lorry on the cross-roads, taking there a back-breaking load of gutted rabbits and hiding only the colour of the pheasants in a well-tied flour sack.

I go into Bangor city. A place for education with its University College, its College where the teachers train, and its Colleges Theological for Nonconformity students.

Dr. Johnson on his tour in North Wales visited the city in 1774. And he had to sleep in a room which had another bed with two men in it.

The cathedral was founded in 525, demolished in 1071, 1211 and 1247, while in 1402 it was burnt by Glyndwr.

And this attack on cathedrals, for he demolished that of St. Asaph also, is a sadness against Glyndwr. But remember he fought oppression and injustice and his years of fight showed his brilliance as a leader. His sons died in the fight for Welsh independence, but Owain himself died, an old, undefeated man, at the home of his daughter.

Glyndwr fought the English who had decreed that no Welsh-man might hold public office and that all the castles in Wales be garrisoned by English soldiers. That if an Englishman married a Welsh girl then he lost all his rights of citizenship and that no Welsh might gather together without written approval first being given. And that no Welshman might bring up his children as scholars, or apprentices to any trade or calling.

A leader the Welsh wanted to give concrete expression to their sense of grievance. Owain Glyndwr, with his own private grievance against the English Grey de Ruthyn became that leader.

In Bangor Cathedral was buried Owain Gwynedd, he who led the Welsh against Henry II in the twelfth century. But he was under order of excommunication at his death from Archbishop Becket for marrying his cousin. And when Archbishop Baldwin came to preach in the cathedral he ordered the Bishop that the body be moved.

A tunnel was made out under the cathedral walls from the tomb to the churchyard beyond. And through the tunnel was moved out the body and the sanctity of the church was restored. Earth and the damp digging under the foundations so that the command of the Archbishop be carried out and the old, unsaintly hero taken away from the quiet walls.

Bangor has its students, and its trains crack to Anglesey and Dublin scented. Bangor remains a place to learn in, sleepy and solid after the tinsel of the gaudy towns, resorts with the brochures and the rivalled hours of sunshine.

Through here are the main routes to Ireland. The Holyhead to London road was built by Telford as a main coach road, now the A5 from North Wales to London.

The road from market town to market town, over the bare mountains or snug through the thorn hedges in the valley, has not the long reaches with trees symmetrical inside little railings. No stern traffic lanes or *Cyclists Ride Here* or *Pedestrians Cross Now*. Even the great Holyhead road becomes a familiar thing in Wales. In the many places mountain and rock do not allow the fancy designing. And there are huddled flocks of sheep walking from farm to farm with busy yelping dog and stick-waving shepherd. In the summer the coloured motor coaches creep by sheep and dog, or fast past farmyard openings, level and open to the road. Squawk of hens in flight desperate from the hum of rubber wheels, the grin under the peaked cap.

The reaches of the country road are kept trim and neat, the sides well cut and the grass scythed level in the summer by the roadman. He who works his length and is known to every house. Coming this way once or twice in the year, working from one end of his length to the other. Working along from the stone gatepost or the milestone which is the start of his particular stretch of road.

In the winter he does the trimming and the gravel sweeping at the sides of the road. Setting a long length of cord taut between two deep pegs and then with his sharp-bladed spade cutting the edge of the grass, and the turf which has grown out from the hedge bank since the last trimming was done. The end of the line reached, and then back to the start of it again and a sliding and levering of the spade under the turf. Slicing it away and throwing the little straggling pieces of clod high to the hedge bank underneath the green grass and the brown bottom stalks of the hedge. And a pride with the roadman never to cut the line with the sharp end of the spade. A steady hand, always, though the cord is waving and humming in a high wind.

Cutting the edge turf and after that going along with a hard-bristled heavy broom. Pushing the long polished handle with the County Council letters burned deep in it, black and possessive.

In the summer the grass cutting. Using a short-bladed scythe with a light handle on the broader verges of the roads. And on the banks and in the narrow places using a bushing hook. Cutting away all the grass and the glory of the dog daisies and the dandelions. Heaping the cut grass speckled with the yellow gilt of the buttercups and the clinging red of the vetches. A line of colour left to wither in the sunshine; and sometimes the particular grass cut which makes the smell of new-mown hay. And from the road meadows the cows lean over with snort and long-reaching tongues.

This roadside hay is free. Some small farmers graze their cows on it, in the quieter parts with the side roads and where the verges are broad and wide. There the cows walk, left to graze all day. With perhaps a boy to watch, or a tired old man who sits the summer hours away on a shaded gate or on the armchair roots of a cool ash. There to watch the cows, to make certain that they do not wander away. A watch and a wait in the afternoon hours until the tea-time and then the slow walk home with a call *bo-hoop* to the night milking.

A memory to me of schooldays and walking home the long, lazy winds of the lanes of Deytheur parish, out of Llansantffraid in Montgomeryshire. Up banks where the melting road tar glistened and which had the marks of the one or two cars tyred in it. And on the way meeting, every summer afternoon, the red of the cows as they pulled the grass with tear and rasp from the wide green sides of the road. And always near them was he whom we called Pugh the Police. He who was tall and thin and held himself straight as the poplars which grew in the half-avenue below the blacksmith's shop. This Pugh who had been a city policeman, a Welsh export to some place in England. Long ago he had retired on pension and the only remembrance of his blue days was the great cape he always wore, summer and winter. That and his straightness and his name.

His daughters gave him this slow job, this watching of the cows. And he had no grumble in him and seemed always happy in the summer, shading his eyes sometimes to watch his cows. Or to peer further into the distance across the Border fields where the hay carts would be creaking and the black dresses of the women hay-makers jerking about like winter crows. He seemed happy enough and we would talk to him under his tree and sometimes he would give us the black treacle toffee. Half-melted by the heat of the summer and wrapped round in many layers of butter paper. He would give us a piece each with shaking hands and would laugh as he would try and get answers out of our full mouths.

He must have missed the summer, old Pugh the Police. Must have missed all the brightness and the happy way the cows pulled at the grass and sometimes looked up at him with their great anxious eyes.

They say he sat by the fire all the winter, in a rounded chair with his cape wrapped around him. I never saw him that way and I remember only the way he was kind to us with his toffee. Kind to his cows for they would pull the grass from under his very feet with never a fear of a raised boot or a slap with the brown hazel stick; the thick staff which he used to lever himself up to his full straightness when rising from his seat by the road.

Grass of the roadside. Sometimes the gipsies take it. They who come with colour and are feared by the Welsh country people. They who come with their baskets and their shawled babies and their dangling ear-rings, bright as brass candlesticks. They come setting up their van on some waste land by the water and travel around the countryside with their little cart. Going from door to door with a half-whine, a half-threat. A hard bargaining always between the farmer's wife and the gipsy woman. And a compromise usually made. An exchange of apples for the clothes pegs or the bright artificial flowers. But that night there is a locking of the poultry-house and a whole length of rope holds the tool-shed.

These gipsies collect the wayside grass. Piling high their cart with it and slipping away quietly with some first July dawn.

The roadman cuts the turf, piles the grass into heaps. Some-times there is the road repairing on his length and a gang come with stone and steam-roller and a surveyor with maps. And once in a while comes the tar-spraying. Once done by a horse-pulled tar-pot with a roaring fire under it. The barrels of tar and the stone chippings laid out at intervals along the road in the months before. And at the time of spraying in the hot dry summer weather the tar-pot had with the group of several roadmen ganged to-gether. The barrels of tar raised to the top of the iron-wheeled cart with a little block and chain. There the bung taken out and the

tar sloshing out into the boiler over the fire. In there made hot
and liquid and pumped out by two of the men at the end of the
long iron handles. The tar spraying out through a long flexible
tube with a rose end, directed by an overalled, helmeted, goggled
man. The tar coming out in a wet shining layer on the road which
had just been swept by men with wide brooms. The tar sprayed
on and the rest of the gang come with wheelbarrows full of stone
chippings from the heaps set along the road. The stone flicked out
on the hot, sticky tar with wrist-flexing twists of wide shovels.

And in the shafts of the tar-pot the horse waiting for the *gee-up*,
to move on a few feet. This horse which is let out to graze in some
farmer's field each night and a shilling paid by the Council.

But this slow way of tar-spraying has gone now. A briskness
to-day, a breath-taking efficiency. A length of road is chosen and
swept by revolving brushes pulled behind an important little
tractor. And after that comes a huge complicated contrivance
pulled by the biggest tractor ever. A long chain of trailers like a
circus or a fair on tour. But no colour here, all is black. And
perched on the trailers are men with hands on levers and feet on
pedals and eyes watching the road and dials and indicators. A
great chimney, too, and a man shovelling coal into a chute. And
every few miles tankers of fresh tar are ready and waiting to slip
into the convoy.

Like some snail this line moves. Going over the many miles of
road in a day. And leaving behind a trail of road covered with
chippings and fresh and bright and done according to contracts,
set and rolled. Only the roadman sees how the edge of the road
has been sprayed too far. And how in the places the green ditches
are wet with tar. Where the greenness will die and a whole winter
of rain hardly wash away the blackness.

Now I shall go to the first of the two islands. Now into fair
Anglesey. An easy crossing over the Suspension Bridge.

Edward I had a plan to cross the Menai Strait with a bridge.
A remarkable idea and only sullen unrest in another part of the
country made him forget his plan. Now where the great Telford
Bridge crosses there might have been an old stern bridge of stone,
lasting out the tides and a monument to military architecture. A
companion piece to the castles of the north-west at Harlech and
Conway and Caernarvon.

A plan to end an island, to make a way into Anglesey. Pass over
the quick tides and the sands and to take away the remoteness and
give the island a new nearness.

Now two bridges cross the Menai Strait into Anglesey. The

Tubular Bridge of great clanging iron tubes which carries the railway across with echo, a tunnel over the water. And the road bridge, the Suspension Bridge, a delicate and spider's web with its dangling roadway.

The Tubular Bridge was opened in 1850. The Suspension Bridge carried the London to Holyhead mail-coach across for the first time in 1826.

The Menai Strait with wood and green fields to the edge of the water. Here where the tides are seen in fast race and where the gulls float white at slack water and the shy sea-ducks swim with ever a watch to the quiet land. Where the sea has a noise and where the sands and the quick water make daring the sail.

Little sailing-boats, week-end pleasure. Venturing out from the leather-chaired clubhouse, top pennants straight in the wind. Sails tiny from the distance, red and yellow and sparkling white. Tilting and a fluttering in the graceful curve as a new wind is caught; a new tack made. And at the back of the boat the varnished wood coping over the little engine which will make the quick ride home when the wind blows perverse, or not at all.

And from the fields the farmers look across to the toys on the water. And carry on stacking the sheaves, the only worry the hidden thistle in the corn heads. The farmers who look up sometimes to the end of the sky in case the wet dark clouds should skim up there, coming hasty on the wind that plays the boats. Rain that will send the yachts chugging to the anchorage; rain that will make mouldy the unstacked wheat, and spare only that which is stooked and through which the next dry breeze can rustle.

I cross into Anglesey, island no longer true, for the true island is reached by boat, and mails and news are all imports into a shy community. Anglesey is an island. But all its remoteness, shyness has long gone. The first name was Mon, called this, The Remote, by the early British. The Romans came and called it Mona.

It was a true island until the nineteenth century, when the only way across the Menai Strait was by ferry. With an eye on the wind and an ear always for the fast tides. Water with a gush, and lovely summer blueness and winter rugged greyness changed to foam-flecked noisiness. A rant and a rave and all the myths and the souls of the despairing sailors raked up from below, there where the daylight never reaches. And where the strange unseeing fish live, fin to mermaid shoulder and the anxious boney hands of the sunken ones wave and waggle. Hands reaching out from the rot and the barnacle of good ship gone, and climbing old bare masts where the last ropes grey and fray before the last crumble, the last drift away. All sail gone and only the sway of the bottom waters to pull on rotten wood, strain old spars.

Menai Strait where the tides rush, and which once made Anglesey an island secure. Its entry a wet journey; the place where the Druids retreated safe at the first Roman coming. There living for many years on the island with sacred worship and the strange-rited hours. In oak grove and with every tree a symbol of the

Divine Being. And the mistletoe not the naughty joy of Christmas but then the sign of dependence. As the mistletoe grew on the oak so were the people dependent upon their god. A queer venerated religion, with the people respecting and fearing the Druids, they who made human sacrifices.

But Anglesey was not the refuge of the Druids for long. The Romans crossed and the island was brought into the scheme of the Roman Empire, supreme sense and law and order. And after the going of the Romans the island became the home of the British princes until the English finally reached all Wales under Edward I.

With the centuries Anglesey remained remote, but with the ferries crossing regular. And when Holyhead was chosen as the packet station for Ireland, Telford built his Holyhead road and crossed the Strait by suspension bridge. In those mail-coach times London could be reached in under thirty hours by road.

And the island was bridged and coming and going was easy, the journey dry.

Anglesey of the low rolling hills, with the white and the grey of the farmhouses. An island with the Irish Sea around and the Menai Strait the separation from the rest of Wales.

I travel around the island. First to Beaumaris, town which I saw across the water from Llanfairfechan. Beaumaris with its castle and its old queer courthouse where the Assizes are held. Men condemned for the sheep-stealing. Here in this little courthouse in the town by the water. Death words and view of the Menai Strait, blue and free as the far mountains of Snowdonia, the black cap, the black cloth and the smooth-running noose.

On along the coast and here is Puffin Island on the east side of Anglesey. A place for birds, a smooth rock lump in the sea. A land loud with call and with the shadow of fast-moving wings in the sunlight. Once a saintly island but no habitation now. In the eighteenth century the puffins were caught and pickled and sent for export.

I travel on to Dulas, to Red Wharf Bay and to Amlwch on the north side. And I pass by Llanfair where the Welsh poet Goronwy Owen was born. He who went out to Virginia and became a minister there.

Two miles from Amlwch is Llanelian where, on August Friday, Wakes were held. And here, once at the time of grave digging in the churchyard, they found the twenty-yard trench with the many bones in it. And they guessed that these must have been shipwrecked sailors of some lost boat. The storms driving and shrieking at mast and sail. Flapping rope and canvas and blowing away spars snapped like smokers' matches. The hours of working and watching and then land in sight. Comes the sudden squall, the sudden end.

On the shore the villagers are watching. Seeing the dancing lost wood and the first grey bodies washed ashore. With the hours and the days they come floating up, are buried. Or perhaps the foreign sailors swim to land. Perhaps are met with pole and scythe. Kegs float up and old lamps. Chests private and initialled with the names of the dead; clothes and sacks of cargo. All are raked up from the sea, dried and shared out. A harvest, the dead gladly buried.

This evil urge, the desire to wreck a good ship, so that the goods washed up might bring a little wealth to the village. Days and nights and the storm is watched with hope that a bare mast might come in from the horizon. A mast swaying with all sail stowed away.

On shore the watchers with an eye on the shoal or the sandbank. Ready to raise the glad shout in the hiss of wind when the ship has struck, all grace gone; with the keel fast and the uneasy list. There out perhaps a hundred yards from the shore with the breakers licking the deck as the tide comes in. And already the nimble ones of this, some coastal village, have gone down, ledge to ledge of the cliff. A search for brass ware and wooden boxes, for the things from this good ship. Timber breaks free and if perchance the sailor clings, then the hands take the spar to the safe shore and the weak one is pushed tottering back to the sea.

Maybe it is the evening when the ship is sighted. Then bonfires are lit and torches are waved to the right way in. But it is only a cleft in the cliff where the ship will drive in safe and all who climb from here can be sent down again into the darkness.

When the storm is gone comes the watch on the shingle, a climb down the cliff rocks. Goods are shared out as the ship breaks up and the cargo comes floating in sudden to the shore with every rising tide. Casks of spirit and bales of strange cloth with a crinkle and a rustle as it dries out before cottage fire.

Bodies washed ashore are hurriedly buried. Perhaps a trench of a grave made along the one side of the churchyard wall, there up on the hill where the stained glass windows are dulled with salt spray. And where on Sunday those on land and sea are prayed for. Those who walk the safe way of the ploughed furrow. And those who love the hum of wind in rope and the disturbed whiteness of a good ship's passing.

Amlwch was once a seaport with all the wealth of bare Parys mountain shipped out.

Those who mined metal in Wales spoke once of *the knockers*.

These the fairies of the underground, who by their tapping lead miners to the richest ore. These were kind, good little folk.

Anglesey, too, is the county where Ifan Gruffydd lost his daughter to a dancing ring of the Tylwyth Teg, The Fairies. She who rashly joined in the dance, slipped hands with the dancing fairies and became one of them, a girl lost to the Little People who danced at Llanerch y Medd in this island. Danced at harvest time, rejoicing perhaps as humans do that the good crop of the year is safely barned. The yield of the year gathered in under one roof or thatch, and safe comes the wildest wind from the sea.

Harvest home suppers are no more and never the joy of the last load brought home slow and heavy in the late summer evening. The lurch of wagons on the stubble fields with the pitchforks stuck wagging brown handles in the back of it. The crunch of the coloured cart wheels on the main road, with the dogs and the up-late children running on to the farmhouse. News that the last load is coming, a flash of white apron in the door and a last quick count of the plates.

The wagons unload, the horses are watered and brushed down. And after that the grand supper with cider speeches.

Now the last load is sneaked home, or taken to the rick in the field corner. A few weeks only and the threshing will be done at the field stack and not in the stackyard. They talk now of the combine harvester, which in the dry summer weather will cut and reap and thresh the corn, all in one clang of cogs, a hot smell of oil and the black spouting smoke of the tractor.

A high-pitched hum across the fields once showed that some farm was threshing. The evening before, the high steam tractor had gone grinding along the road pulling behind it the threshing box, red and square. This latter with inside of it the rollers and flails to thresh out the wheat and the oats and the barley and send it trickling out through spouts at the back. Iron spouts fastened deep into sacks which were bowled away to the granary when filled.

The box would be set up in the stackyard and the steam-engine away and in line so that the great flapping belt should all day run true. Run from the gleam of the big engine flywheel to the main drive-wheel of the box. This started and its whine would echo the countryside and all knew that to-day it was the threshing.

And men *followed the machine*. A set occupation this, going with the "machine" from one farm to the next to help work the threshing-box. Men on top of the stack to throw the sheaves to the top of the box drawn up level with the edge of the stacks. And on the box, a cold, draughty place with dust and noise, would be the two men. These handled the sheaves, one with his hands, the other with a short-handled pitchfork.

The man with the pitchfork would catch the sheaves as they were tossed to him from the top of the stack or barn. Catch them nimbly on the bright sharp points of his pitchfork. And he would carefully and quickly pass them on to the other man, he who was on his knees with the square leather cushions strapped around them. The leather padded inside with soft stuffed cloth and used at the times of ferreting and at the times of threshing to take away the ache from the points of the knees. Special farm gadgets and still used, like the thick leather gloves to handle the hedge thorns when a *gap* is repaired and at the time when a high prickly hedge is pleached and laid low.

The man on his knees catching the sheaf thrown to him always with the heads of corn pointing in his direction. He then using a short, sharp knife and cutting the string binding the sheaf and pushing the splayed-out corn down the opening of the chute and into the revolving drums and beating machinery. This man whose hands are hard and calloused, with the many specks of the little thistles from the cut sheaves deep and grey and brown specks in his hard skin.

The sheaf going in from the top of the box and the grain coming out through the spouts at the back. On one side of the box is the chaff, the soft husk from the heads and stray little straws all shaken out. And at the front end of the box comes out the loose, long straw stalks with the little cut lengths of wiry brown string; the string which is collected and tied into a long, loose ball and used for the odd tying jobs on the farm throughout the year.

A rattle and a whine, a noise and dust always at the threshing time. In the house the farmer's wife anxious and worried at all the extra catering. And in the stackyard the hens are pecking and raking the straw for the loose, stray grains.

The straw was piled on one side and used later for litter for the cattle. The chaff was used as pig litter or kept and mixed with cow cake or other feeding stuffs as an emergency feed for the winter months. Cow Cake and Indian Corn and Thirds and the other animal feeding stuffs which come to the farm in the sacks and are. emptied into wide steel bins as a protection against the rats. Fattening foods and food for the milking cows and Indian Corn for the chickens. And the meal and the bran to make the hot mashes for the poultry and the pigs in the cold weeks of the year.

There were the accidents at the old steam traction and box threshing. He who was on his knees would sometimes cut his fingers in the cold weather with his razor-sharp knife. His hands

cold and numb and for a time afterwards the golden stalks going
head-on into the heart of the machine would be red and smeared.
For they would have fetched him a cobweb to put on the cut and
a strip of an old torn-up sheet to wrap around his fingers. But the
blood would ooze out and there could be no leaving the place on
the box for fear that some other man might take over this honoured
coveted position. This man was always exposed to the most danger. Sometimes it was from an inexperienced one behind him who,
in his eagerness, might drive the points of the pitchfork into the
back of him. Or that in a strong wind the dust might come up and
blind him so that he would lose the feel of the sure boards under
his knees and topple in among the grinding cogs. That happened
sometimes and shout then and the man at the engine would pull
away the flopping driving belt with his bare hands so that the
machine might stop. Then it would be a mangling, a loss of arm
or leg.

Sometimes men had their heads caught in the belt as they
dodged under it. Farmers with the risk of accidents always, at
threshing time. And at harvest time when there might be a fall
from a stack or a tumble headlong from the hay cart when the
horses move unexpectedly.

The threshing is a quicker business now. No waiting until the
middle of the winter and no need to get the sheaves under cover.
For the corn of one field is now stacked high in a corner and a
waterproof tarpaulin is thrown over to keep off the rain. There in
a few weeks comes the little Diesel tractor with its small box and
baler and elevator. All drawn up neatly to the side of the stack.
The tractor spurts and runs all the day with no attention except
refuelling. The box is low and has the safe guards. And when the
stack is near the ground there does not have to be the high pitching
for the little petrol-driven elevator raises the sheaves to the top of
the threshing box.

The bags of corn are filled and are weighed on a portable scales
and then labelled and loaded into a waiting lorry. Taken straight
to the railway station ready for the mills; with no need of a cool
granary for storage and the wait until a fair price makes a worth-
while sale.

The loose straw is passed straight to the clanking baling machine,
is compressed into neat handy bales and tied under pressure with
wire.

All is done quickly and efficiently and perhaps while the threshing contractors are yet finishing the stack the farm's own tractors
are making brown with glistening furrow this stubble field. The
earth turned over and its richness made ready to give again in

green, re-seeded pasture or in straight-rowed, green-topped root crops.

I go on to Holyhead where the steamers go the fifty-five miles to Ireland. This the port for Ireland since early days and this way came all the travellers to Dublin and to London. Laced and frilled, with wig and knee breeches, buckles bright and heads powdered. And with ache of journey in every noble bone.

Holyhead, this end place of Wales, yet even before the telephone it was possible, by visual signals via Prestatyn, to send and receive messages from Liverpool in half a minute.

This the link port with Ireland. And it was the Irish of the Conway Castle garrison who were tied back to back and thrown into the river. This by order of Mytton in 1646 when he took the castle.

The railway company now maintain the service, prompt and efficient to the blarney western world. Pause at Holyhead, and sniff as the boat comes in. For perhaps Irish air lingers in hold and cabin. Exciting air and finding Wales a land of chapel and farm. With wildness and freedom only on the sides of the bare mountains, and on the wilderness waters of Cardigan Bay.

I leave Anglesey, this island joined to the mainland with cunning construction. But the island still has a remoteness about it. A bare country with the feel of the old sacred days still there. When the mists come and the farmhouse seems unknown in the winter twilight. With light in some window mellowed, or made clear by some swirl of wind. And then only a glow again, far away and with frightening shadows on the drawn blinds. Reflected profiles, unreal and ghastly, black in hideousness and with a raised hand having all hate. And in the mist the toll of distant bell, the moan of distant buoy. Or the annoyed hoot of some ship, in from the Indies and delayed here, with Liverpool and dock and home and wife only just over there, through the fog.

Sometimes in the night the fear comes and the catch of breath, the prickling sweat, sudden and hot. The look over the shoulder on the moonlit road or the peep from warm sheets to the frame of the windows. A look back along the road, the shadow of the trunks black and the mushroom heads of the bare-branched trees reflected quiet. Or a look out through the window, half over land, half over sea. Times when the schooldays come back and the stories of the Druids. Priests moving in sure certain ways with the old certain rites. The people watching and trusting and believing that this was the only truth, the only religion.

The mist, the road in the moonlight and the view of the night through the window. Perhaps some old call, some phase of the moon, a slant of the sun next day. Day for the old rites and the worship. But to-morrow will be only the cars and the visitors and the ships steaming by. And with gleam of silver wings, planes for Ireland. So perhaps the old ways are postponed, or just go on unseen. And with only the strange feel of the night or the mist to say that they are coming. That to-morrow all will be over and done with. There will be sleep sound for all the island, with the roads safe for little children, safe to play hide and seek in the shadows of the trees. With sleep sound for those who woke uneasy last night, and even the curtains are floral and gay in the sunshine with the yellow blind tucked up on its roller at the top of the window. The shadow is only Dad stretching his arm to the warm of the fire, or Mam putting in the old polished hair curlers, a safe use for the night.

I start again from Bangor city. Down along the Strait and the way to Caernarvon. I meet the boy pedalling the bicycle, his body side to side with the urge of his pushing. His hands centred on the handlebars and dangling there by a short white piece of string the brownness of a fox tail. The brush curved up and around and the tip fastened loosely to the black enamel of the cross-bar.

The lad pedalling the road, anxious and hurried. Taking the prize home, or to some shed of boys.

He went by. I did not ask him where he had come from, where he was going. For the end of the brush was fresh and red where it had been cut away. And the white of the string was smeared with an untidy redness as the fur swayed with the speed of the bicycle.

Foxes come down from the hills to the valley poultry. And on the moors and the mountains of Denbighshire and Montgomery-shire, Merionethshire and Caernarvonshire, the foxes catch the young lambs in the early spring.

The fox comes to the unfastened fowl-house and next morning there is the trail of feathers, white across the meadow fields. Or the orchard has the headless hens, all blood sucked away.

The fox to the sheep and the lambs. Often choosing the ewes with two lambs, for the defence of one is always easier. A lamb snatched and the bleating, long-legged whiteness carried away.

A deep hole for lair, under the roots of some old tree or on the sunny side of the mountain, where the cubs come out to play like big gnawing puppies.

In the valleys the foxes are killed by the Hunts. And on Saturday afternoons by gangs of farm workers with shot-guns and farm dogs who go up to the mountains for the foxes.

All a sad business, anyway, and necessity made the excuse for the hunt, the grand piling-up of odds against. But barbed wire, the intense cultivation of the land and the changing social way of things are ending the valley Hunts. The colour of the bright suits; and the bay of sniffing dogs on a cold morning, are still seen in mid-Wales and some of the valleys. The last of the landed gentry, and gentlemen farmers with time to spare from tractor-sitting and the farm office.

Up in the hills the fox-hunting is less refined and the sporting chance is reduced to an accident such as nightfall or mist or heavy rain, or an awkward shot peppering somebody with pellets; hot and the blisters ending the day's work.

There are two methods of mountain fox-hunting in North Wales. The one a drive across the side of the mountain. Beaters calling and slashing the gorse bushes and the bracken in a long line. The sheep-dogs playing with each other and with none of the nose for a keen scent. Foxes are often cornered in this way in a drive across a mountain and then there is the shouting and a rush to be first in with the shot, the final bowling over.

The other fox hunt is the holing method. The fox has gone to earth, or the lair has been found and carefully marked. Then comes a digging out with spades and a careful watching. And towards the end a rod of iron is pushed in. A stout rod made by the village blacksmith and with a sharp, up-curved hook at the one end of it. This is pushed in and generally the vixen bites and is hauled out with the hook fast to her mouth. A hitting of spades and the kicking and trampling of heavy farm boots. The warm body is skinned. The brush cut away and a thin, stout string tied around the fleshy end of it. The skin is cut and loosened, the string held by one man and the brush is slid off by another. This done like the peeling of a glove from some white lady's fingers.

The cubs are dug out and round furry heads flattened with the high-raised spade.

The lambs are safe again, the day's sport over. And with the grey of the afternoon the men go back to farm and valley village. Spades over shoulders, the steel rod red with blood, and hot water and sandpaper the job for the back kitchen evening. In the light of the oil lamp the brush is passed round with a joke to the women. The young ones laugh and ask for the story of the afternoon. And only granny refuses to smooth the fur in the mellow light. For she is from the old days, and holds that foxes are for the gentry only.

I come into Caernarvon town with its narrow streets and its castle where the first Prince of Wales was born and where William Prynne, commoner of the time of Charles I was tortured. He who had his face mutilated and spent the solitary hours in a quiet tower of this majestic castle. But later set free and becoming a member of the Commons, with his burnt cheeks and the roots of his ears left witness to intolerance. Pain and misfortune where now walks the wide-eyed tourist, the secure sightseer.

The castle was built in the thirteenth century by Edward I as part of his castle-building policy to subdue the Welsh. The castle had many sieges, being attacked by Glyndwr, and later becoming a shuttlecock in the times of the Civil War. Afterwards an order was made that the castle was to be dismantled and ground-levelled, yet it escaped this and only the inside accommodation was taken away. The rest of the castle remains, with its thick galleried walls and thirteen high towers, one of the finest castles in existence. Imposing on its acres and preserved now as a grand specimen. Town walls, too, were built to Caernarvon by Edward I.

The town is on the Menai Strait where the River Seint dies into the tides after rising on Snowdon side and forming the Llanberis Lakes. The river lost, pacifist and gentle from the blue-remembered mountains.

In Roman days Caernarvon was Segonium, an important Roman station.

Caernarvonshire has always been the last refuge in the battle of the invaders. Its mountains and alpine lakes and its uplands, places to hide in and easy to defend, sweet roughest Wales.

Now those who live in the mountains are only a short ride with car and trailer from the valleys and the coastal plain. Telephone reaches the upland farm and drooping mast and sagging aerial bring radio to the many. But still some of the older childless couples will have no music but what comes from the little harmonium in the front room. Or from the yellow ivory-keyed piano with its fret and silk front. Rosewood kept polished and face reflecting and with tall brass candlesticks hinged to the front of it. Still in the sockets are the candles which are lit when the once-in-a-while hymn-singing comes on a Sunday evening. And the old lady whose hands are stiff and her fingers awkward, her skin hard with work and the nails broken away with all the outside farm work, she plays. But first she has to soak her hands in warm water and after that rub in the vaseline. Does this so that her fingers may have some of the old suppleness and the tips of them be able to reach out easily for the black keys.

Her husband sings and in her unlevel voice she joins him. But it is cold in the front parlour, and the way the candles flicker brings all the old pictures on the laced piano top to life. The waving yellowness over the miniature, long ago painted of the grandfather. He who had been one of the gentry until the law had gone against him and the suit had been lost.

The two of them leave the parlour for the kitchen. That is lived in and all china, every wood, has a familiar feel, a friendly smoothness.

Once on a sheep farm I found the spinet. Square and dignified in the front room opposite the old Welsh dresser, carved and black and brass-handled. On the dresser the dull pewter with the ruby china set in between the plates to give a gayness.

And across the room, tight against the wallpaper was this spinet. The square case closed down over the keyboard and the whole flat table-top of it bare and polished. No photographs or souvenir pottery, no crotchet mats. No samplerwork, that slow, coloured and complicated embroidery seen often in Welsh homes, initialled and dated and a souvenir of spinster winter evenings, or of young, uncourted girls' empty nights. Work slow and eye-tiring in the light of rush candles, but work now treasured and hung on wall, or tilted on table top.

This spinet, they knew not where it had come from. Except that it had been long in the family. And did they play it? Oh no, it was awkward and there was too much of a tinkle to it, like the old piano in the Village Hall.

But all of the spinet was dusted. All of the keys were kept clean. And as I struck a little of the sharp sweet music I felt that here it was best left quiet and still. For the front parlour with the heavy dresser and the staid pewter was not the place for gentry music or maidenly hours.

For life is work for the children of the upland farms and growing up with a wonderful view, the sun on the hills and the changing colours mean little. A day in exciting Liverpool the thing to look forward to, or to the towns of the coast with the Sunday school trip in the hired motor coach.

Rolling clouds, white in the blue wind, or black with the first drops of rain, these taken for granted. And it is the cinema and the expensive dancing legs, the softness of plush seats, these are the thrilling things. The crag on which the climbers go in the summer is idiotic and a foolish place to venture. A steep, dangerous place and when the sheep drop there it is a time for police and ropes and a certificated reward. A swing over the swaying depths with trust to the hands and the deep-driven stakes above. Not a thing for pleasure. And done anyway in the working clothes with none of the breeches and thick stockings, none of the tools and hanks of rope of those who come from England to climb and strain. A sheep to be rescued, nuisance that she is, and a pendulum must swing human to some awkward ledge.

The mountains are home to the lads of the upland farms. And the market town is the thing of excitement. A place to wear the second best suit and to be hushed and quiet.

Sometimes sons leave the mountains and the valleys. Perhaps

too many sons at home on the farm and the wars call and there can be no agricultural exemption. Or perhaps there is an urge to leave, and this is a good excuse to go. An uncle has a job waiting in distant Liverpool, in the drapers' shop or on a milk round.

The son goes away, a new way of life is found. City houses have wheat flakes for breakfast but the bacon has a dirty taste. Bread and milk is the food for invalids or those who have had all their teeth out. Tablecloths can be dainty with colours and fancy designs. And in the city chapels the deacons are business men with not the domination of the chapel fathers back home. Back kitchens are called sculleries and do not smell always of paraffin and the coal goes straight into a cellar from the street. A whole new way of life, with noise and people passed and seen, and never passed again. With coffins going through the streets fast with none of the country slowness. And never a person stopping to raise a hat or stand quite still as the funeral goes by. The cemeteries are not bare little corners on the hillsides but great farms of places. With trees all around and acres of whiteness; and a hay harvest in the summer, while at home no man would gather the hay between the mounds but leave it to wither and die and no disturbing of the dead.

Sons go, the city lights calling. Sometimes the daughters go, often to that favourite calling, the nursing. Coming home with dreadful stories of suffering ten times worse than anything Job had to go through.

Then there is the going to college. An ambition that son or daughter should go to college, get letters after the name. Important that, the letters. So that all the village and the neighbours talk about Tom B.A., or Caradoc B.Sc., or Idwal the Doctor. The best choice, perhaps, is that the son or daughter should be a teacher. Not the Irish longing for the son to be a priest, but if the boy does have the "call" and does enter the Ministry, well, that is a blessing and though there is not much money in it, well, it is a credit to the family.

Up they go, gilt-framed or oak-edged, the photographs on the mantelpieces, the diplomas and the certificates on the parlour wall. Reverenced as a testimony that our lad has done well. That our girl has kept herself above reproach.

Perhaps she will come home as a teacher in the village school. Or to be blue, cycling, black-bagged, district nurse. And the son who is in the ministry, who has the chapel living many miles away, perhaps some Sunday he has the engagement to preach in the home chapel, there where he went to Sunday school and where on a Sunday evening he had to go with all the other children to the front of the Big Seat to recite verses. Sometimes a verse and a hymn and the minister, when he has finished his sermon, coming down from the pulpit and listening. Perhaps asking a few questions.

The Welsh minister. He who lives in the house near the chapel. Sometimes the manse is joined to the chapel and the curtained windows are jolly by the long narrow round-topped windows of Salem or Ebenezer or Zion. But maybe the chapel has only a little house joined to the back of it, a path iron-railed and a latched wicket to say *Chapel House*. There where lives the caretaker and his wife. The man to keep going the central heating and to light the fire in the vestry at the times of the deacons' meetings. The man who rears the sliding ladder with squeak and run of cord pulley on his half-day, a cleaning of the tall bare windows.

The woman who for a day in the week cleans the chapel. A washing of the steps and a scrubbing of the blue mosaic tiles inside the porch. A dust of every pew and the coco-matting taken up once in a while. Taken up and hung over the clothes line for the quick beating. A polish and a filling of the brass-bowled paraffin lamps. A wind of the big white-faced clock stared at by all the preachers as they fill the allotted time each Sunday. The clock with the loud, even tick and which at every hour gives a sudden click and ping, for they have taken away the mellow gong which told the hours when the clock was in the Hall kitchen. Bought there at the time of the sale and given to the chapel by the newly-made deacon.

The woman cleans the pulpit and dusts the Bible and the hymn book there. Sets carefully the red tasselled cloth which dangles over the edge. The cloth which is always red, except at the times when one of the chapel members has died. And then the red cloth of the pulpit is covered with a black cloth for several weeks. A custom this, a sign of mourning.

The woman dusts the organ and opens the top half of the windows with the long cord. Opens them in the week middle and closes them in good time so there shall be no Sunday draught.

The minister lives in the manse, the name of the house strangely foreign in the village. And only sometimes comes the ardent Welshman who changes it to some Welsh name, painted new and bright on the front door.

The Welsh minister is a man of importance in the village. He who has charge of perhaps three chapels of the same denomination in three neighbouring places. And he has to cycle the distance to the various meetings in the various villages. The minister of one of the other denominations lives in one of the other villages. A mutual arrangement so that several ministers shall not live in one village, and that there will always be one ready for the funeral, the christening.

Many of the villages have three or four chapels as well as the church. There is little co-operation and hardly ever an amalgamation for service.

The ministers black-clothed and white-collared who are on the parish councils and who organise the Eisteddfodau and the concerts. And between the vicar and the Free Churches there is a constant bickering. The vicar often refusing ministers to conduct the burial services at those of the chapel dead who want to be buried in the churchyard rather than in the village cemetery. And at the Armistice Day service at the village war memorial there is always an argument as to who should conduct the major part of the service.

Most of the chapels have a system so that the resident minister only preaches in his own chapel once or twice in the month. For the rest of the Sundays other preachers from other areas, near or far, come to hold the services, preach the sermons. These ministers generally come by car, sleek and smart and easy from fifty miles away for the ten o'clock morning service.

But still some of the ministers stay the week-end, the older ones and those who have no cars. For the trains are inconvenient in the Welsh valleys on a Sunday.

The few ministers stay the week-end, carrying on the old custom. Once the preachers came on horse-back or even walked to arrive in time for Saturday night. Staying the week-end with one of the chapel members and preaching on the Sunday.

Each of the chapel families takes a turn to lodge the ministers. A grand airing of beds, white lengths of sheets and the folded-over feather mattress before the kitchen fire. And even when the bed has been made the old flat irons are heated up and spread three or four about the bed. For it must be aired for the preachers, and only the best will do. A fire is lit in the front parlour where this month only in the year is the match put to the local paper wrinkled up below the brown old sticks. The best ham is taken down and a supply of tobacco bought, kept cool in an earthenware pot. And if the preacher known to chew, then a little hard twist bought as well, hard and black and liquorice-solid. The good fire is stacked up and the best armchairs drawn up squeaking on unoiled castors.

The minister comes on the Saturday afternoon, often in time for tea. And after that going to the front room, to talk, to tell the stories, to smoke the pipe, to toast the toes evangelical.

At ten o'clock comes the supper. After that the family prayers, for when the minister stays in the house there has to be worship. The minister, with a last suck at his pipe, or a last brown spit into the fire, opens the family Bible and reads a few verses. Then on his knees to pray with the lamp turned low and only the light of the fire, red-coaled, peat-glowed. The clinker drops in the pauses between the sentences and there is no *hwyl* here. No great dam of reserve broken down and every fervent thought allowed to burst out with shout and fist and tear.

Prayers over and then the minister talks with the man and woman of the house far into the night. Talks of the old days, the sad new days, old happy memories, new first-told experiences.

Getting to know a preacher and the preacher getting to know the families. Ways of eating and the bare moments in the home life, bang on the plate and the whispered word through the half-open door.

And *hwyl?* This is the word of emotion in preaching or praying. When steady, calculated oratory breaks down and the emotions charge every word. A great torrent of speech with the acting arm and the tear in preacher and listener. Amens like a whip from the congregation to make the preacher rise to new more fervent heights. All infectious and the congregation and the preacher piling up emotion and shuttling it the one to the other.

Old men remember the Revivals when religion swept in a great emotional surge across Wales. And men stopped ploughing in the valleys to kneel in the soft furrow. Women sang hymns at the butter-making. The chapels were crowded every night with the prayer meetings and there was a queue up the aisle. Life centred around the ugly stone chapels and the Revival meetings were all-night sessions. A race among the new converts to be the first to read the Bible from black cover to black cover. The old saints nodding from the Big Seat, safe with fifty years of prayer and five or six readings of the Bible.

A signing of the Pledge, too, a campaign against Drink and Pleasure and Carnal Joy. The puritanism lingers on to-day, the distaste for the village pub, the local dance, and the girl with the child born out of wedlock. She is "cut out" from membership of the chapel. *Man is frail and needs a constant whip*, the minister flays the well of the pulpit, *a constant whip and an ugly good woman is more pleasing in God's sight than this, a beautiful bad woman. Close your eyes to beauty people, let ugliness be your guide.*

There can be no heckling, for the minister is cock of the pulpit. The good-looking Welsh servant girls look solemn and only the mind laughs. The black hair still twists and curls and the elf eyes laugh brown from the blacklead eyebrows. The chapels make old women saints, and only hags are the godly ones. But love and youth shimmer under it all and the façade cracks with the young men home from the fighting.

Once every Sunday in almost all the chapels is the Sunday school. There where people once learnt to read and an institution which has done much to keep alive the Welsh language.

To the Sunday school in the country districts go the young and the old. Perhaps there are one or two classes for the children and some half-dozen for the grown-ups. In charge of the children is the minister's wife or some convenient school teacher. The teacher in charge of each of the older classes is generally a deacon. The children often have their classes in the schoolroom if the chapel is large enough to have one. There the children go with their noise and their chewing sweets to sit around a stove or a fire. There to learn to read Welsh, first the alphabet and after that the various little booklets special to each denomination. Catechisms and the fundamentals of the religion set out in question and answer. The older children read Bible verses. Each Sunday each child has to say a verse and a hymn to the teacher. These are entered up with the record of attendance and at the end of the year a prize is given. All members of the Sunday school have this record set against their names, a list of attendance and of verses said. There is a book prize for the child and the adult who says the most new verses in the year. Also each year there are whole books of the Bible set for learning out, a few verses at a time, to a specially appointed listener. He makes a report and at the end of the year an illuminated certificate is awarded. Scripture examinations are also held each year, when printed question papers are set and the answers have to be written out in a strict examination session.

The children go to the schoolroom and the adults to the separate classes in the chapel pews, a few seats left spare in between the classes. Verses are first said and after that the Scripture portion to be examined that day is read. The teacher stands in front and then comes the arguing and the discussing and the threshing out of theological questions. Arguments over some specific word. Commentaries on the Bible are read in the week before and the various modern translations into English are studied. But the bringing of Biblical aids to the Sunday school is disliked and a sign of poor knowledge.

The Sunday school starts with a short service. Ends with a general catechism of the whole school. The deacons take it in turn to question the school on the Sunday's lesson, and everything ends with prayer and the bowed heads to the hard, wooden, varnished front of the pews.

The inside of a Welsh chapel is a bleak place with straight, wooded pews. A pulpit set central at the one end with steps to go up to it. Below is the Big Seat where the deacons sit starched in glory. A reading desk is usually in the centre of the Big Seat and this with a Bible and hymn book on it. Flowers seen only in the city chapels and the remote country chapels of North Wales have a bleakness and a bareness. With the only comfort allowed is a self-bought felt cushion to take the coldness and the hardness away from the seats. The pews are numbered and have little hooks or a hole in front of each seat to hold the individual Communion cups.

The windows are long up the sides, with the bottom panes frosted, religion made bathroom private. The ceiling is plain white, no fancy painted cherubs or buxom angels. In one corner, or under the pulpit, is the organ. In the country a simple affair with the wind got from the desperate pedalling of the organist. By the organ is the pew where the precentor sits, he who starts the singing and picks the tunes.

In the chapels they have a worry known as the *devil of the singing*. This is the never-ending rivalry between various singers to be precentor, and among all who can play the organ to be the official organist. A compromise often tactfully made and a rota of precentors is drawn up for the months of the year. And the organists have alternate months, or share out the playing at the services. Only at the time of the Singing Festival does ill-feeling really arise, for who is to play then when all the strangers come and the important conductor has come from the South? Then the deacons arrange for a guest organist from some distant village. He or she who has the letters after the name and who perhaps gives music lessons teaching village children to play the piano.

Every village has its collection of chapels, strung out along the one street. Severe buildings, iron-railed and long-windowed, bare of all outside ornamentation and only a stone set high to say the name and the date of erection. No flower beds or lawns on any of the unused surrounding ground; there earth and weed, or paving stone only. But the paintwork of the railings is always kept fresh and bright, and the sweet papers and cigarette ends which have blown in from the road are swept out each week.

And out in the quiet country roads, in a field corner or set in the trees of a little roadside coppice, are the chapels for those away from town and village. With always stables at the back, most of the country chapels have these for the use of worshippers who come on horseback or in seldom used horse and trap.

In many places some of the village chapels have had to close. Supporting families have died out. Or there has been one of those major quarrels which happen often in Welsh Nonconformist life, and many have left to join another denomination.

The deserted chapels are locked up and perhaps after many years they are sold. But a good time lapse is always allowed in case the "cause" should come to life again with the coming of a strong religious family to a farm or in retirement to the village.

The chapels of Wales. Pass on a Sunday morning and hear the fervent singing, the little organ wailing. Or pass at the time of the evening service, lamps making yellow the height of the windows, arched at the top and unstained, curtainless. These places which are the social clubs and the community centres of the Welsh people.

And the Church in Wales? Most of the parishes have Welsh and English services. The churches are always lovely, sweet hallowed places with the old walled churchyard and no harsh iron railings. A peace and sanctity, with the old striking clock, the lovely simplicity of the Norman arch, the heights of green ivy. And inside, all the beauty of old glass, filtering in the sunlight in rich mellow colours. A place to take hats off, to tread quietly. The font round-smoothed and the roof rich-raftered. And the feeling of all the others, too. Those who have passed on, but have beauty to rest in.

Centred in the village, set at the end of a shaded path and shadowed in tall elms and beeches and dark with the weight of old green yews. Some village churches with a great acreage of churchyard, a sign of the old ecclesiastical importance of a particular church. Some with the rare circular churchyard wall. All the parish churches of Wales are full of antiquity, the centre of the religious life of the parish before the coming of sere Non-conformity and the building of the grim, gaunt chapels.

Church bells sweet-toned and engraved with motto or message or challenge. A favourite is:

"I to the Church the Living Call,
I to the Grave summons all."

Many of the bells from Welsh churches were cast or recast in England, often being taken to the Border and sent down the Severn. And many of the bells have English inscriptions on them, and often more to the glory of the local Welsh squire than to the glory of God.

Bells ringing wedding and funeral and national occasion. The bells of Kinnerley, a parish of the Border country but situated in Shropshire, have a sweetness due to the generosity of a farmer. And the story is worth recalling, though the bells ring out over flat farmed Shropshire.

This farmer had sold two of his best cows at the Shrewsbury market and was on his way home when he passed the church where the bell-makers had set up a portable forge to recast some of the bells. Someone asked him what was his contribution to the cost of the new bells. And the farmer took out his handkerchief full of silver coin from the sale of his two cows and emptied it into the molten metal of the furnace. The bells cast, it is said, have a sweet bright ring.

Often to my home by the sea the wind brings the Sunday morning pealing of the bells of Barmouth Church across the mouth of the estuary. Ringing louder, ringing softer as the wind ebbs and flows across the little waves of the tidal water.

And once in a while the sound of a shot-gun, striking across the pealing of the bells and echoing inland from far up the estuary. But there is only a little wild fowl shooting. And that only the amateur effort of the visitor or half-day tradesman. No decoying and camouflage clothing here and the floating birds are safe in their hundreds. These shy ones who can be seen quiet and unafraid as a train passes, but who fly fast flapping-winged into the sunset when walking boot crackles the marsh sedges. The flying teal, all colour lost in the blackness as they rise to the west, quick and anxious.

Sometimes a holiday-maker shoots the oyster-catchers. These are not over-shy birds and even a cunning schoolboy, by manœuvring and crawling, could kill on the sands and mud-flats with his catapult. These hard-working birds who poke with orange bills in the wetness after the tides have gone out, and who in mating time trill and pipe through the night. Their call and the lap of the sea against the wall the only sound through the lowered window. Day-time they fly, grumbling and complaining, low over the water to new, fresh, wet sand or mud-flat. Skimming the water and sheering away from some jutting-out rock where a fisherman is perched, his hand-lines out to the incoming water.

The sunsets on this west coast, viewed from this last loneliness, are incredibly lovely. After a blue summer day the sun sinks away red and moon-round in the sky. With all the reflected light making red the mountains of Cader Idris and giving rose colour to the drift of clouds as they move in from the sea. Their whiteness taken away and a new unreal colour delicate and clear against the darkening evening sky. The clouds drift far back into Wales and only when the sun has quite gone do the old colours come darkly back for the night.

Down the seventy fertile miles of the Lleyn Peninsula, this remote land with its little red sands, its shingle coves, and cliffs bright with long-lasting gorse and heather ledges. Little trees sloped and stunted and arched away from the prevailing winds, strong from the sea.

Here perhaps came the smugglers, to cove and inlet, for the Welsh coast was the scene of a considerable amount of smuggling. Some of the shore houses have communicating tunnels and many are the shaped paths across the meadows to snug coves on the sides of the estuaries. In Stuart times there was much salt-running from Ireland to evade the salt taxes. And some of the church vaults are said to have been regular storage places for smuggled goods. And who knows now what ships slink over from the west or south to the lonely estuaries and the little sandy shores?

Coming perhaps in fog and in secret, and waiting until the wind blows away all mist, so that there can be a safe landing at the arranged, quiet places.

Fog, the private thing. When shore and rock take on new moving shape and all noise loses echo, anxious gull and the boom of the barrier. The distant train whistle becomes a new note, and far-away talking becomes near, and then is lost again. And the wind blows rent in fog and a new shape to the top of the trees. The golden sand greys with the wetness and the pools that the tide has left behind have no sky reflection. The green of the crabs crawling side to side, stone to stone, has an excitement, a colour. White sticks from the sea can be seen now in all their bone and rib pattern, for the eye cannot lift to mountain and sea and sky. Each near stone has a shape, and white veined marble gleams life and colour.

A house window lighted and yellow loses form with the drift of the mist. And through the lavender bushes new phantom shapes move, with never a rustle of the small sharp leaves. Never a pause to remember scented sheet or heavy-aired distillery.

The moan and complain of ship is not heard often on this west coast in the fog of the year. The red-sailed yachts are safely har-boured and the little pleasure boats are upturned undignified on the quays. Wet with paint and all board to be scraped and sealed again.

Not often this fog to the lonely west waters. But the dull air has yet the tang and taste of the sea. Seeping skin and cloth, but a

clean, good thing with none of the factoried grime of city blackness. This fog comes up healthy and robust from the Irish Sea.
Creeps in between the houses of the little villages and the small
towns on the side of the sea. Creeps through street and drapes eave
to eave. Doors are opened and shut quickly and hands rub before
the fire-grate bars. Rub of knuckle in the rounded palm and a
blow of breath noisy through the teeth.

The lifeboat crews wait half an ear open for the call of the rising rocket as it shoots over the town, sign for the calling together of the crew and signal that a distress has come in. Some stray ship lost or those who have come floating in rubber dinghy from some aeroplane. All to the boathouse and the winchmen are waiting. The winch knocked open and the boat slides down the specially fitted slipway to the sea. Or maybe the boathouse is away from the water and the lifeboat has to be towed through street and over sand by a tractor.

Signal and search and home again. Tractor through the streets or the boat hauled up the slipway by the winch. Fog and sunshine, wind or the cut of snow, all times the rocket high over the town is answered.

Mermaids play in the sunshine? Or perhaps it is in the moonlight and the quiet time of the fog that they come out to sit armchaired in the gullies of the cliffs? Or play hand over hand in the sand? The fog makes private the open places and allows the unbelieved ones to come joking out, to clown and play in the places which only moonlight and fog make safe for them. They who laugh at hook and at those of science who have explored all sea bottom; listed who live there, and indexed all that they have seen with calculating eye and felt with cold, reasoning finger. But ask the farmer who has walked the cliffs in the moonlight in search of his lost sheep-dog. Or ask the poacher, he who walks the shore way to the salmon river up in the hills. Or ask the fisherman who was late on his journey home, the wind perverse to his sail and the petrol motor broken, only the pull of his oars to make headway.

Ask them, for their eyes know the shape. And their hands know old signs to keep away the frolics of these, the strange, unreal ones.

The shepherdess of the ocean, she who controls and orders the waves, she is said to be a mermaid and her name Gwenhudiw. The little waves are her flock, each wave her sheep. But the seventh waves which come in crashing great, these are said to be her rams. She is always urging the sea to possess the land, for she is not content to be shepherdess of the ocean only. But she wants her kingdom wider, and her dancing sheep to cover the acres which are now dry and green and rooted.

Once down the Lleyn Peninsula came all the pilgrims with hope to the Isle of Bardsey, for this was thought to be a more worthy venture than a trip to Rome. Down this way which is now green farmed and fertilised to a yielding soil.

And on the west side of the Lleyn is Nevin and the heights of the peaked Rivals.

Nevin where Edward I had a great jousting tournament as a final triumph at the end of Welsh independence. Lords and ladies

from England, and beyond, to play at the sports of war and to make happy pastime in game and feasting. A show for the subdued Welsh, an exhibition of armour tough and ladies beautiful. Of the power of the English Court; its fame abroad. How the invaders could make fun on as grand a scale as war.

And in these present times, with the wars, camps and aerodromes have come to North Wales. Farms have been taken, homes old in generations of families. Flat fields have had their hedges taken away, and old houses have been surrounded by stark, red-bricked buildings and black, round-roofed shanties of galvanised iron. Where the sea slopes down from the highlands of Wales to Cardigan Bay, there on the west Welsh fields they have built camp and parade ground. And in the mountains and on the moors they have taken land for practice fighting and for testing gun and shell. The towns of the coast have the English troops, good natured and joking at Taffy and the song of his voice, the shy ways of his women. They fill cinema and café and against them there is no ill-feeling. But they who erect camp and commandeer farm in Wales must expect bitterness. A heritage is taken away and to the Welshman of the mountains his farm is more than a business proposition which a Whitehall cheque can buy. Generations have lived and died in the same stone house, generations of Joneses or Evanses or Watkinses. The farm is not a shop which can be locked up and forgotten. And there has never been any retirement from it. The old have been born there and they will be carried away down the same stone lane where they learned to walk.

The patriots stir and protest and petition. But the Welsh lack a national leader, spokesman who can unite the North and the South. For the North of Wales and the South of the country do not co-operate. A feeling in the North that in all national matters Cardiff is too remote, too anglicised to deal efficiently with Welsh matters. And on committees and planning schemes the North and the South representatives have a habit of presenting differing viewpoints so that an inquiry is satisfied that there is no national wish on a specific matter.

Another land, almost, the South of Wales. The Welsh who come up to the North can hardly be understood, and the Welsh who go South, likewise. They who live in the remoter parts of North Wales claim that their form of the language is the purest, with none of the alien influences of the Border country and of the valleys of the South.

The fervent Nationalists campaign for the preservation of the Welsh language. Advocate its compulsory use in schools and in official documents. But there is no national theatre for performing plays written in Welsh, and the readers who can be reached by a Welsh novel are few. And the cultural activities of the National Eisteddfod are in many ways curtailed by the academic outlook of the purists. The young Welsh actors then, work in the scope of the English stage, and the authors write for the wider English audience. For the Welsh creative artist, like all others, is concerned with the breaking down of barriers and the reaching of individual hearts, everywhere.

The Rivals are high on the west side of the Lleyn Peninsula. These mountains which were hated by sailors who would not venture near this part of the coast. For it was said that the ironstone in the mountains affected the compass and gave an evil bearing. Sailors who were not afraid of the long dancing wave or the shell-shaped white horses as the sea sucked over the rocks of a known channel. But fearing these mountains, these peaks. Here on the west coast of Wales where the wet west winds come in from the Atlantic to the land of Wales. Depositing some of their rain on the coastal area. And then as the winds rise to cross the mountains more rain falls, sixty to seventy inches of it every year. The mountain centre of Wales, from Caernarvonshire down to the south is a watershed with mist and falling rain. Soft penetrating drizzle to the heavy drumming rain which demands the last button fast and the head bent forward. Rain to soak the bog and make a thousand tiny waterfalls, twisting silver in the brown and green mountainside. Trickling and pounding and a straight fall to join some mountain brook as it twists with spray and cold wet moss the short way to the sea on the west. Or the longer ambling way east, a meander into England.

Springs of the mountains, bubbling and boiling from under a dark slab of rock. Or rising clear in a little precious gravel on the side of some hill. With the grass around a brighter green, and the new stream gushing anxious away.

In summer the little streams of the mountain sparkle, and in August sunshine birds ruffle feather and wash in the stray pools shallow in the rock. The grasses bend long and fresh and the water moves clear, save where it has come the peaty way. Sheep, the unthirsty animals, come sometimes in the late evening or the early morning for the rare drink. And when the shepherd rounds the sheep the dogs come panting and hanging-tongue thirsty to the fresh water.

In winter with the heavy rains the streams lose their tinkle, a roar comes and the rush which has carved stone make certain shapes down the mountainside. Comes the snow and the way of the stream is left bright and black in the whiteness. And only when the snow melts comes a muddy roar, shaking the bank grasses and soaking the boulder moss.

And the wet mists of the mountains. A lost, frightened world with crags alive and shaped as the mist rises and falls, drifts away and thickens. When the sheep huddle wet fleeced under the ledges and only once in a while comes the bleat, muffled and far away. Or a curlew calls, high above the mist.

Mist which soaks the cloth and brings a cold ache to the long bones of the body. A chafing rawness to the ankle where the boot edge rubs wet, and a pain to the eyes as they strain to see the path, the drop, the way to the valley.

The edge of the mist reached at last. And there with the first farms of the valley is the rain. Pounding on slate roof and making a gurgle in the landers and the down-spouts. Filling the black barrels which hold the soft water for the next washing-day. For the water of the house has to be pumped by hand. And it is hard water used for drinking only and a difficult thing to get a lather with. On the farms all the washing is done at home, with the laundry vans calling only near the towns. But often the special things are taken into market town to the laundry. Things such as the starched hard collars and the best white tablecloths.

But the rest of the things are washed at home. All the underwear and the overalls of the farm men. All the sheets and all the towels and the blankets. The smocks which are used at milking-time. And the white muslin which covers the butter basket on market-day.

All are washed with the rain-water. The water boiled in the washhouse, a small covered building with a boiler in a corner of the back yard. There a steam and a sizzle and the warm smell of damp clothes. With one of the servant men leaving the farmwork for the day and coming to help turn the mangle. A red-hot face and the joke with the servant girl when the missus goes to the house to start the meal making.

And the clothes line in the orchards from apple tree to apple tree. Held half-way along with "Y"-ended props. Long white and coloured lines of washing pegged and raised high above the rooting pigs and the scratch of the hens. A flapping and a great cloth-shaking as the wind dodges around the big trees. With whip and whirl, the wire line fast to the tree trunks. Fastened there all the years and the scar of the fixing has been grown over with bark and the end of the wire is deep and far away in the very sap of the tree.

Then there is the ironing and the mending and the airing. A few of the farms have been modernised and have bathrooms and hot-water cylinders and airing cupboards. A few have the electric power for the irons. But for the most it is airing of the clothes on great hangers wound to the top of the kitchen, or on a bright brass wire above the range. And at night it is the clothes-horse propped before the fire.

The ironing has to be done with the old flat-irons. These are clamped to the bars of a hot coal fire and heated. Then a rag is wrapped around the handle and a shoe slid quickly on. The ironing has to be done briskly and while the other iron is heating. Some of the moderns have portable gas irons and some use a hollow iron filled with charcoal blocks heated in the fire. These are picked out and packed into the hollow space, a lid fixed on and the iron used.

On Saturday night the piles of clean laundry are placed on each bed. In the front bedroom where the farmer and his wife sleep, next to the best bedroom where the preacher sleeps at the time of lodging. And in the back bedrooms where the farm men sleep. And where the maid has her bolted room. Dingy little rooms with iron bedsteads and the wallpaper curling away at the top corners, drooping and mildewed with dampness. Where the furniture is an old marble-topped washstand and a white cracked jug and floral, unmatching basin. And a wardrobe, perhaps, or a row of hooks curtained off in one corner. And always under the bed the great square box. This the private treasure chest of all Welsh farm workers. Where all the worldly goods are kept under lock and key. A tin chest with the owner's name painted on the outside in careful, shivering letters.

When the farm girl or man changes his place in May, then this tin trunk is moved. Bowled away squatting on the handlebars of the bicycle. Taken away from one farm to another at the time of *changing places*.

The hiring of new servants is fixed by word of mouth and a few shillings passed over at the time of moving. And the promise made is always kept.

So in the scented nights of May, when the days draw out and

each night brings a shorter darkness, then they move, the farm workers. I meet them in the evening, puffing and pushing their bicycles along the slow slopes of the roads. With the tin trunk held firm, one end on the handlebars. A good-bye said to the farm which has been the home, week-end and week for the last twelve-month, or the last ten years. Left now perhaps because the food has gone bad; or because of a sudden row with boss over the state of the top stackyard; or just because a change is wanted. And it is the precious bike, the chief worldly joy of the Welsh farm worker, which moves the "Things". To the hope of a better bed-room which has no rag-filled broken pane. Or to the hope of a breakfast broth which has not the splinters of bone to annoy the teeth. Or just the longing to see the length of a different cowhouse each night and morning. To spread manure in new fields. Or to warm the wet winter hands before a new kitchen fire.

Housewife on the mountain farm in Caernarvonshire or Meri-onethshire, the uplands of Montgomeryshire or the Denbigh moors. She who picks the blackberries, staining and soft, from the side of high lanes where once the Romans straight marched. Or picks the elderberries black and hanging and ripe for the winter wine from some woodside. A slope where Glyndwr once halted with a look to the view and an open eye for the glint of English armour. The housewife who gathers crackling morning sticks from some dip in the land, there where the fairies dance; she who gathers morning sticks from fairyland. The housewife who takes in the old dirty-faced woman from the village, she who has the glint of ear-rings yellow in her long lobes. And who they say is a gipsy and her distant father a Spaniard. A great ship wrecked at the time of the Armada and her distant father, many generations away, he was the only survivor. He swum from the ship and was thrown up on the Welsh coast rocks and made his way inland. There he was accepted and there he married. And all the descen-dants have the swarthy faces which no pumice or Persil will remove. Not that she who they call the witch ever uses pumice or Persil, for she is a little mad as well as dark skinned and fears a cold if she should ever wash in water, no matter how hot. But she can speak Welsh and swear in other tongues besides. And she is the best woman in the whole valley for daily help, not caring how high the farm is in the hills and able to scrub floors all morning and wash up the crocks without a finger mark.

Housewife who still polishes with beeswax and turpentine. Who makes bread, white and light and with a crunchy brown crust. Who can deal with a whole sheep killed, or the meat from a great fat pig.

A hobby and pastime on many of the lonely Welsh farms was furniture-making; settles and chests and stools. Many of the North Wales homes still have this family furniture in the house. With the old black marks of the rush candles on the top of them. There where the rush candle was stuck, intended for a moment only, but forgotten, and the candle burning away and finally scorching the wood. These rush candles were made from the pith of rushes, the outer skin peeled away and the brittle inner pith dipped into fat, generally mutton fat saved from sheep-killing. The rush was dipped and allowed to dry, and afterwards dipped in again until a thick layer of fat was formed around the central core of the rush pith.

The chests were often elaborately carved and went with the bride when she left home, full of linen and dowry. And with a smaller compartment inside made of fine wood to hold the more precious part of the gift.

Walking sometimes in the mountains I have come upon the thick grey walls of an old disused farmhouse. Built snug in the hollow where the ridge of one mountain slopes down before a higher rise.

Wide foundations of boulders waist-high, and with the mortar hard and uncrumbling. The farm buildings joined to the one end of the house and wild plants and scraggy fruit bushes in the garden at the back. The house roofed with small, thick green-grey slates, with round clumps of moss and lichen on the slope from eave to ridge. Welsh slates up to about 1750 were all of a small size and after that other shapes were introduced called Doubles, Countesses, Duchesses, and Queens.

This old house with its windows black spaces to the inside. And the doorway closed up with a rattling, rusted sheet of galvanised iron, white with the droppings of the perching birds nesting inside.

Side to side of the door little strips of earth, bordered with even white stones and edging the slabs of rock which floor the yard. Garden perhaps of some child, or woman who wanted plant and bud and colour. All green-tangled now and white with bursting thistle heads.

This peasant farm which was not enough of a livelihood to support the family. Or perhaps there were no children to carry on and a neighbour bought the land and let the house go to decay. Or maybe the landowning squire added the land to the next farm and decided that the small house was not worth modernising, and anyway who would want to live in the mountains with only view and sharp air, but no acres, no sheep-walk?

I go to Aberdaron at the tip of the Lleyn Peninsula. Village with the long far view to the lonely sea waters; the sea which makes a solitude of Bardsey Island.

Aberdaron is famous for its Dick, Richard Jones, Dick Aberdaron as he is known and remembered in Wales. A queer genius of a tramp of the early-nineteenth century. The son of illiterate parents and teaching himself to read Welsh and understand its grammar. Before he died he was a master of thirty-five languages. Yet all his life a dirty, unwashed, care-free tramp. With no love in life except the learning of languages. A wanderer in England and in Wales and pity taken on him many times by scholars and by clergy and by squires. He in his filth and rags allowed to live in some stable or out-house for the strangeness of hearing him spin out Hebrew or Italian. This man with a knack of the learning of a language. That only, and with no love of literature or the understanding of a foreign way of life. An interest only in basic grammar.

Dick was buried at St. Asaph. He had a huge funeral, and even now Dick Aberdaron is a wonder in Wales. This man who hid dictionaries between his skin and his smelling cloth. And who would make friends with any for the happiness of learning a new language.

The last headland of the Lleyn before the waters of Bardsey is Braich y Pwll. A high cliff and a gallery to sit and stare at the magic of Bardsey. This island which was once the great pilgrim centre. Sit here and remember all the hope of the pilgrims, all the faith for Bardsey. Peaceful now, the Lleyn Peninsula with its farms, its dreamy lanes. Its cliffs to the sea and views pastoral from the windows of the farmhouses. Slow hills green for the farmers, and the sea for those who fish from the coastal villages.

The wars have brought camps and the screech of diving planes. This warm land which I can see from my house, see from the top of the hill which rises behind home. A land blue and kind in the distance. On the south side of this land there is now a great holiday camp, shuttling the thousands every week. But from my hill only the mist and the blue and the outline of the Lleyn shows, with the raised end of Bardsey Island at the end of it. With the view which I can have any time from my hill, the view across the bay and I lose the greenness of the fields, the white meeting of rock and sea, the shape of barns, the clump of a tiny village. The distance of my view across the sea gives me the remote Lleyn.

But this is not the distant, ever, view. Here are the last miles of my journey. And here is Bardsey.

The island is three miles from the mainland, three fast miles of sea. At the north and north-east side the island rises to a mountain, the edge a cliff to the sea. Ledges for the sea birds, safe homes where rope and swaying body only can reach the nest.

The soil is clay and gives a good farming growth. But the winds stunt high shrubs, blow small the deep-rooted tree. And they say that there were no sparrows on Bardsey until the early-nineteenth century. One family came then, the first of many.

And the graves, these twenty thousand saints?

Digging by the old abbey once they found the many graves, lined saintly with clean white stone, reverent until the long-nosed diggers came, those who live only for dust and urn and bone. With bone and urn and dust no more sacred than the strong gold heart of a mountain. Things to be dug up, dug out. Turned hand over hand in the daylight, stored in a cardboard box at night. Anxious prodding spades and academic fingers which stir white in the remains of the dead. They who make dry the past.

The first Abbot of Bardsey made an arrangement with the Almighty that his monks should die in order of seniority. So that each knew when his time came, and could prepare himself fully for his end. Each to go in his time, unconcerned, unworried. For it would be the oldest who would have to next go. The good Abbot made this pact with the Lord on behalf of his pious monks. So that their days should not be worried, and the time of their going known.

Islands are always full of longing, of the people who want to go there. Bardsey is the island of the Saints and the Seals. The saints, twenty thousand of them; the seals breed in the little caves, play in the sunshine on the low-tide ledges.

A fast tide, foam flecked and twirling, runs between the island and the mainland. A dangerous crossing and the island sometimes forsaken, and then inhabited again. The school is seven now and the island is 370 acres. The people are farmers and fishermen and a stray poet or two; keepers at the lighthouse and those who visit the island, and hurry away again. For the noises on the island are unknown and strange at night. The sea birds calling, the gargle of the sea in the rock gullies. The suck and the tear and the flopping water. And the wind blows off the Irish Sea with all the old ships moaning, the lost sailors laughing at the light of the dancing lighthouse. Winter and the winds and the tear of the sea. Summer and the quietness and the little sounds echoing the island.

And all around is the sea. The twenty thousand saints hemmed in by the ever-moving fence.

On the north side was once St. Mary's Abbey, founded in 516 by Cadfan. About the seventh century many refugee saints came here. Coming down the pilgrim way of the Lleyn Peninsula, to die, and lie for ever, on Bardsey. Island of the noises, island of the sea. And land proper a whole dangerous boat-ride away. To-day the motor boat takes the food and the mails, the lighthouse keepers and those who are sick.

The battle is on, always. Some day the urge to leave will come again. The stone houses will be left to the wind in the winter days, the bats in the summer nights. The lighthouse will flick over the empty island. The boats cross emptier, and only once in a while.

An uncertain place to live, Bardsey. With only the summer sunshine and the loneliness for compensation. Sunshine and loneliness go bright and well together. But there is more storm than sunshine on Bardsey.

I go along the south side of the Lleyn. The way that goes from Aberdaron to Pwllheli and Criccieth and Tremadoc.

Out of Aberdaron and by Hell's Mouth Bay, the untempting name for a lovely water. This bay has always had the bad name among sailors. For in old days not only was this an evil place for ships, but for shipwrecked sailors as well. The people on the shores had the hard hearts and never rescued ships' crews; never helped those who tried to land. This an easy bay to enter but a dangerous place to sail out of. For it is said that the winds always blow strong into the mouth of the inlet. And that the tides, no matter whether rising or falling, allow always the top current to rush in. So that there is no easy return to the open sea. A dreaded place in the days of sailing-ships. A fear of Hell's Mouth and of the inhospitable ones who lived on this edge of the sea. A ship to them a treasure and a fortune sent into the trap. This place a safety from the gales of the sea, but once in, no going out again.

Sometimes, perhaps, a young good-looking sailor allowed to land, the heart of a Welsh girl full with pity. A courting, a marriage. The foreign one accepted into the life of the village.

It was the custom in the mountains in the eighteenth century and early nineteenth for the Courting on the Bed. Not Courting *in* the Bed, for there was a wickedness about this.

There was an excuse for this custom in a country where there was no privacy in the living-room and the only lonely places were out on the side of the mountain or in the farm buildings. The valley people were luckier with their gentler weather and shaded roads and snug buildings of the larger farms.

But the young men and women of the mountains wanted the comfort and the quietness together. And so Courting on the Bed came. Not an immoral thing but a matter of convenience. Children seldom born before marriage. A date was fixed and the young

man came to the girl's home in the early evening. Then hiding
outside until the family had gone to bed and the signal came from
the young girl's bedroom. A wave of hand or a low whistle. The
young man then finding the open door downstairs and an easy
way up. Or a climb up the wall with reach and pull at a dropped
blanket. And there the Courting on Bed going on through the
night. And if the young man was forward, or anxious over the
separating bolster, then there was the smack on the face or punch
on the nose. His bad name told to all the neighbours and the comfort of bed courting gone from this young man for all time in the
district.

A snug, happy business and seldom spoken of in stern, Nonconformist Wales. The chapel with high hands in horror at such
a temptation. But perhaps on a cold night in the mountains still
the young man rides bicycle or drives car to the house where she
lives. And perhaps a window still opens, the cold glass squeaking
back and all the stars reflected at the invitation. A wall is climbed
with a ladder from stackyard or outhouse. Or a downstairs door
is shyly opened and the first breathless words spoken. And at the
end of it all a scrambling down the ladder at the five a.m. good-
bye. A hurried last wave. A carrying of the ladder to its proper
place and a scurrying home on bike or in car for the morning
milking time. With only a sleepy head and bad conscience to deny
all the questioning. A shake of the head, such things have died a
hundred years ago. And at forty even the guilty ones forget;
these are old oats, old foolish customs. All best forgotten.

But Dad locks the ladder in a stronger barn. And last summer
he changed her bedroom to the north room. Away from that snug,
warm room which had all the setting sun, and the great pattern
of the pear tree clamped firm to the whitewashed wall below.

On by St. Tudwal's Bay and Abersoch to Pwllheli. This town
once was a shipbuilding centre and had a flourishing shellfish
market.

There were curious phosphorescent lights seen at Pwllheli towards the end of the last century. Of varying colours, red and
blue and rising over marshy ground. Watchers who went out to
them reported them as human shaped, tall, and moving over the
surface of the ground. Coming in from swamp land and swirling
round the gable ends of barns and houses. Previously in 1694 there
had been exhalations at Harlech, these mentioned by Evelyn in
his *Diary*. These took the form of blue flames which burnt hay and
straw and could be dispersed by the blowing of horns. But the
grass became so poisoned that animals died while grazing. It is

recorded that a short time before this a plague of locusts had visited this part of the Welsh coast and died, the whole shore being covered with the bodies.

These strange lights were believed to have an association with death and the visitation of spirits. Dogs are said to have knowledge of near death and many are the tales told of faithful dogs howling before the death of their master. And lights dancing across the fields from house to churchyard, house where that week death comes. One recorded story of a farmer waking one night and from his window seeing a shaft of wavering light going from a neighbouring farm to a certain place in the churchyard wall. He and his family and his servants seeing this light. And only the next day came the news of the death of their good neighbour. But more to the story, for snow came and drifted so high that they were unable to take in the coffin at the churchyard gate. To make a way in they had to demolish the churchyard wall, and that was done at the spot where the farmer had seen the light touching on the death night.

Before death there comes a desire to most of the country people to have the Last Rites, a partaking of the Holy Communion. After a long illness, when the many months have passed since the last rite was partaken in chapel, then there must be again a new sacrament before death.

In the Welsh chapels the ceremony is extremely simple. Few use now a chalice, generally it is the individual, delicate little glass cups, bright red with teetotal wine. For none of the chapels would use an intoxicating drink. In the early days of Nonconformity the communal cup was used, but that has been laid aside now. But yet the bread is broken on a silver plate and the old tradition of giving the consecrated left-over bread to the birds is observed. But there is no majestic organ-playing and no robed clergy. A simple hymn is sung, unaccompanied, and two of the deacons take around the bread and the wine.

The minister visits those who are ill in the home. Visits them when there can be no hope of recovery. The only view the slope of the hillside through the small-paned windows, the colours of the last days; the silence of the long last nights.

The Welsh have always a preoccupation with death. People die at home in the lonely houses, where there is not the satisfying nearness of the houses orderly in a city street; where there is none of the whiteness of the hospital, place where the humming lift going up passes the dead going down to the ground floor mortuary.

People die in the mountain farms of North Wales by lamplight. In low-roofed bedrooms with the black shadows of the watching ones like great hunched birds on the yellow whitewash of the ceiling. And an oak beam up there giving an extra horror to the shadow, a wing or great thick tail. Or some bony elbow transformed to a great birded beak. The lamp has been brought up from the kitchen and down there they move with candles and a kettle is kept rattling on the hob, for any time now the hour must come and the district nurse will want hot water. She who does the last offices, although some parishes have the layer-out, she who does all such work in the district, being not a qualified nurse and only a visitor to death rooms. Places where the sun is kept curtained out and slants in yellow in the little openings between wall and curtain edge.

The woman makes the shillings with the laying-out. And the job gives her an eminence in the village. She and the carpenter-undertaker and the minister, they who are in touch with the dead are more important than the district nurse who brings lusty babies into the world, or the registrar who writes marriage lines in his slow, square way.

But some of the narrow, twisting farmhouse stairs have never known a coffin. For the length of the polished wood could never twist in the narrowness, never be reared gently by the neighbour bearers down the steep steps. In such houses the very sick are always brought to a bed set up in one of the downstairs rooms, a place from which they can be carried easily when the time comes. And they who are ill know this, that this setting-up of the bed in the downstairs room is a sign that never again will they walk the hills, watch the black race of sheep-dogs.

Old shuddering thoughts. A fireside evening of tobacco and spit, and cigarettes lit with fast-burning, snap-sparking splints of dry wood from the logs at the back of the fire. A winter evening I spent when the snow was on the ground and day and night there was that stillness which comes with the whiteness. The local vet had been called out to a farm high on the valleyside. He was a man for company and I, on my way to the evening post, had had to go with him. A journey quiet through the snow with only the noise of the loose skid chains on the back wheels. Out of the village in the evening, the indistinct time when snow clouds hang low all the day, giving early night. Out of the village along the white roads, with the traffic marks deep and rutted in the hardening snow. Sometimes a man leaping off his bicycle in the half-darkness and standing ankle-deep in the side snow until we had passed, headlamps making more unreal the fantastic drifts, and snow concealing familiar shapes of the road.

To this farm to the calving cow. A freak, a sport of nature, and this calf had the four front legs and unable to be born. The vet operating with little knives held in the palm of his hand and after that using a long, specially serrated steel wire with smooth handles at each end of it. This a kind of saw; a desperate business so that the cow might live, and the loss be only this freak, this unholy combination from the hereditary root of things.

After that the antiseptics and the supper; the talk around the hot kitchen range.

There the tales turning to ghosts and goblins and things that fly low in the night. A talk for a winter evening, for this New Year snow. When ear listens to the spoken word, and all the body waits taut and expecting the other noise, outside.

One said that night that the worst noise he knew was the coffining. The time when the undertakers come carrying awkward their empty shell, covered with the black cloth. Taking it upstairs and setting in the body.

It is the walk of their feet on the ceiling, said he, *it is their walk and when my brother died I thought sure I could hear the three pairs of feet on the ceiling. But it was only Shone and his mate.*

The old man in the corner said that when he was young they used to go to the village church on the night of All Hallow E'en. Go there and speak in Welsh at a particular window to the spirit who was there waiting. And he would answer back and give the names of all those who were to die during the next twelve months in the parish. And the old man said, too, that in his time people were never allowed to die on a pillow or on a feather bed. We asked him why? A time this for such talk, what with the year gone and snow outside.

The old man told us that people could not die easily if there was a feather of a wild thing under them. So always the pillow and the bolster and the mattress were removed.

"Rosemary for remembrance", says Ophelia, and this herb was used often at Welsh funerals. Each of the mourners was given a sprig at the house and all wore it in their buttonholes, and after the last words of the priest all threw their sprays down into the open grave. A funeral to which I was taken when very small, after the last words of the service had been spoken, after the rattle of earth as the sexton cast his handful of soil, then the relatives dropped sadly in little nosegays of rosemary. It had seemed to me to lack the colour and the majesty of the great floral wreaths, for I did not understand then that rosemary was for remembrance.

The old Welsh had a reverence for this plant and folklore said that it only blossomed at Christmas time.

In the eighteenth century bodies were buried in canvas in Wales. Material shaped like the old bricklayer's wallet and two coffins were kept in the parish, one large and one small, and these were used as biers.

After the funeral the sexton would make a collection around the grave, using his spade as a collecting-box. One tale is told of how the local wag had his joke. For the sexton sometimes would reach over the grave rather than walk around. And the wit, placing his money on the flat blade of the spade, pressed to the one side so that the spade turned and all the collection went tinkling away into the grave.

Funeral cakes were always given. A recipe for a batch was: "Mix twenty-four beaten eggs with three pounds of flour and three pounds of grated lump sugar. This will make forty-eight cakes for a funeral."

Superstition and a belief in the uncanny. Relations who bake bread each week. They who have their own wheat ground into flour and at one baking producing a week's bread for the family and the farm workers. A special oven used, opening out into the back kitchen, an iron door waist high, and shelves inside to hold the flat loaves pushed in with the broken, wooden hay rake. And before each lump of dough is slid in, untinned and the bread all oven bottom, then a mark is cut on top of each piece of dough with a knife. And the mark is still the mark of the Cross. I ask them why they make that sign on top of their bread, that holy sign, for are they not staunch chapel folk and not agreeing with papish practices? But they do not know that it is the sign of the Cross that they are making, they thought it just an old fancy design, the same that mother had made; and her mother before that, doubtless to pre-Reformation times.

Still there is a belief in the country districts that the best medicine for all ills is consecrated sacramental wine. A cure for all diseases and a wonderfully potent healer.

Sawyers once travelled from one saw-pit to another. With great two-handed saws doing the work which now the power-driven circular saws do quickly. One of the worst occupations, to be bottom man in the saw-pit, with all the sawdust falling. The local Tom the Sawyer who died the other year, he had gone quite blind and his married daughter told us all that it had been the dust falling on his face all the years, for he was one to keep looking up, she said. And wandering about the country lanes, his stick tapping the hedgerows, he was even now looking up to the sky, blind, in his nineties.

I had never the heart to ask Tom about the curse. For it is said that all sawyers are under a curse for it was a sawyer who had to prepare the Cross for the Crucifixion.

Beliefs and faiths, a trust in odd things among the Welsh country people.

Cinder tea used for many ailments in babies. A hot cinder dropped into a tittle hot water and the infusion given to the baby to drink when the district nurse has closed her black bag and gone.

Small-pox was cured by making an infusion of sheep's dung flavoured with nutmeg. Patients cried out for this remedy and it was also extensively used in the treatment of measles.

The seventh son believed to have a healing power and many a mother has gone in search of one when the local doctor has failed to cure the whooping-cough, for the seventh son is said to have a rare power to cure this.

And toothache, that which comes often to the Welsh country people. They who are not over keen on dental care and a regular bill at the dentist seems much waste of money. And anyway a visit to the dentist means a half-day wasted, a special journey to the market town. The teeth only come out on doctor's order or when the pain throbs for days and nights. I know of the farmer who has risen in the hours of the night and walked the sloping fields and first mountain acres of his farm. And he has gone to bed again in agony and bent long over the one side of the bed so that the blood may rush to his head and ease the pain.

Charms were once used for toothache in the days before frosted glass windows and bright brass plates. Here are translations of two charms:

"St. Mary sat on a stone, the stone being near her hermitage, when the Holy Ghost came to her, she being sad. Why art thou sad, Mother of My Lord, and what pain tormenteth thee? My teeth are painful, a worm called Megrim has penetrated them and I have masticated and swallowed it. I adjure thee daffin o negrbina, by the Father and the Son and the Holy Ghost, by the Virgin Mary, and God the Munificent Physician, that thou dost not permit any disease, dolour or molestation to afflict this servant of God here present, either in tooth, eye, head or in the whole of the teeth together. So be it. Amen."

"Get an iron nail and engrave on it Alga-Sabaoth-Anthanatos, and insert the nail under the afflicted tooth. And then drive it into an oak tree, and while the nail there remains the toothache will not return. But first you should carve on the tree with the nail the name of the man afflicted with the toothache, repeating the following. By the power of the Father and these consecrated words, as thou enterest into this wood, so let the pain and disease depart from the sufferer. Ever so be it. Amen."

The magic is believed, ghost and legend. The tale of Gwrgi Garwlwyd who was said to have eaten a Welsh male and a Welsh female each and every day. But on a Saturday he killed two of each so that he would not have to spill blood on a Sunday.

And death is more news than birth, or the ways of life itself.

I go on to Criccieth with its castle and salty view across the bay. This castle which had once Hywel of the Battle-Axe for its constable.

This Hywel y Fwyell fought for the Black Prince at Poitiers. And was so dexterous with his axe that he was made Constable of Criccieth Castle, and also of Chester. He was also granted the weirs and fisheries of the coast and charge of the King's Mills. He was knighted and a more lasting memorial was also given him. For every day a portion of meat was given to the paupers of Criccieth with eight soldiers to guard it. And it was only in the reign of Elizabeth that the custom was ended. This meat was laid out before the battle-axe which had done service at Poitiers.

Each village has its butcher. He who stands blue-aproned by the white marble slabs with his head among the redness hanging from the bright steel hooks. He who wears the short white coat, with the twisted apron string around his middle. And who, in the spare hours when the customers are not in the shop, cuts meat on the scarred wooden bench. Little chippings of bone and stray slicings of meat arch to the floor. The meat lost in the red colour of the bright tiles and only the white bone showing, a crunch to the feet.

The butcher who is a deacon, sober and bowler-hatted on a Sunday. Or a soft-footed churchwarden. Always a man of importance in the Welsh village. He who before the grading and central buying came could go to any near farmer to buy the lambs, the pigs and the one fat bullock beast a week. And the shop was closed always in mid-week and on Wednesday and Thursday nights came the killing. The slaughterhouse in some lane of the village with only a red drain to the slow river to show the use of the place. This building which was once an old malthouse. Or a stable in the days when the doctor had kept a groom and had ridden the country roads in a high dog-cart.

Only the drain, and once in a while the stained lorry from the tanner's yard in the market town coming to collect the skins and the hides.

Friday and Saturday in the butcher's there would be the dangling carcases, the ropes of hand-made, peppery sausages, and the white oval trays of black puddings. Village people and those from the big houses coming for the week-end joint; the hotel for the saddle of mutton.

A big whine, now, in the village butcher's shop and the children from the Sunday school tea party have ice cream from this refrigerator, a white glistening pail of it, and the meat is killed and dressed in central abattoirs and comes sacking-sewn in a covered van. The middle of the week are idle hours for the village butcher, for he will not go to be a slaughterman in the depot in town. Saying that their ways are rough and ready and that there is no art in their killing, no skill in their dressing. And that their hands are not tender enough to carve firm, juicy meat.

The village doctor, son perhaps of a thrifty Welsh tradesman, goes away to Liverpool or to Edinburgh to qualify. Comes back to Wales, for the Welsh-speaking doctors are popular. The old aches and the ailments of the family can be explained easily and quickly. No halting language, no translation, no useless flapping of the hands when the right word does not come. Welsh people are not over-fond of doctors, the country and farming people especially. People who have never known the cold rubber and metal of the doctor's stethoscope, or the dials and switches of the X-ray apparatus. Who eat an unbalanced diet and who know nothing of the value of vitamins. Yet well in health and able to work all day at thistle-cutting in the drizzle of rain. Or able to sweat at the walking behind the one-horse plough and afterwards sit eating lunch under a tree, with a cold breeze never giving a chill to cooling body. Farmers who live in houses with no bath-room and only an earth closet. And those of the villages where there is no sanitation except for the night refuse cart organised by the Rural District Council.

Hard living, easy dying. And the pain must be the pain of the years and it is only when the fever comes and bed a happy thing that the doctor is fetched. Ache is borne over months, a tumour or perhaps it is that dreadful malignant growth which swoops on the healthy countryman equally with the sooty man from the city. Pain is carried for a long time and it is only when disability comes that there is the visit to the dim-lit, leather-seated village surgery. There in the cold waiting-room with the door that does not quite shut and where the dead leaves blow in, on and under the table. A brownness among the torn, glossy magazines and a piling-up against the ash-grey stove in the corner, there where the rain has made rusty the once black-leaded pipe.

A horror, too, of hospitals. Not so much at the helplessness of a ward number, the cold efficiency of a confidential case sheet. But rather the worry at the distance from home and those who can speak Welsh, the distance away from the farm and the sheep and the old familiar food.

North Wales in its remote places is not a happy place to go suddenly ill; only two modern hospitals in all its counties, one at Bangor, one at Wrexham. And in the specialist cases it has to be the specific hospitals on Merseyside or in the Midlands. A frightening journey among the trams and the dust and all the many people. Home all the parish know of the ill, the disaster which has come. Always the gentle-hearted question asked, news of better or worse. The neighbours come to help with the milking and the next farmer sees to all the buying and selling of the stock for the market. Distant relations come and all the Welsh good heart helps in this time of trouble.

The end comes, perhaps, in the city. Far away from the fresh wind and the view of the scrambling sheep on the mountainside. The village carpenter becomes the undertaker. He revered because of his association with the dead and because of his importance at the funeral time. Dai the Carpenter who has had the many strange things happen to him in the forty years of burying. The many times when he has found the two pennies on the eyes of the dead. Coins heavy and cold and put there by the relations after the last hour so that the uneasy stare of the eyes shall be taken away. Coins left there until the coffining and it is Dai who has to decide what to do with them. But when he was an apprentice to his old master, he who is still spoken of as the best coffin-maker for miles, and holding the record for speed as well, it was he who told Dai what to do always in such cases. Consecrated they are and slip them into the coffin, boy. But wrap them so that the bearers do not rattle them. Don't want the coffin to be a dice-box, boy.

And that way it has always been.

Dai tells the other tales, too. Half sacred, half of the Satan world. Of corpses which have grown. Of Rees who had conducted the village orchestra and who had willed that his fiddle, in strict tune, be buried with him. And tales, too, of the cats and the frogs and things laughed at by those of town and city. But listen to Dai among the shavings and the pitch and the shaped boards and all his tales defy doubt. And walking out from the village under the dark of the fir trees, with the moon on the sea, all magic can be believed and all mystery be told around the next stone bend of the road. There above the sulky sea and the flat-stoned shingle and the sand and the lost black strands of the sea-weed.

A look now to the mountains of Caernarvonshire. Sometimes on a warm spring night when curtains are drawn back for the night air there is a redness seen on the hills, a moving line of fire. And the smell of burning bracken and gorse.

They are setting fire to the rough mountainsides. The farmers doing this in early spring so that all wasted growths shall be destroyed and only the fresh grass roots grow quickly and unhindered.

The time is carefully chosen, after a day of calm wind and gentle sunshine. One of those first spring days when there is a green urge in all trees and a new look to fields and hills.

Then the dry bracken is lighted, the places carefully picked so that the fire shall not get out of control. And if much height of fern and much tangle of gorse is to be burned then narrow trenches are dug across the mountain sides to limit the fire.

Days and nights and the hillside burns. Red to the evening sky and black acres left. All sheep are cleared away and with crackle and smoke the unwanted growth flames away.

Stand by a window, watching through the blueness of the night, across field and quiet valley up to the mountains. Stars flick and before the morning there will be early frost and shoots in the garden will be nipped and to-morrow's sunshine warmth for dead plants only.

The Welsh are not keen gardeners. Those of the valleys and of the warm coast, they have their shows and their allotment exhibitions. But up in the mountains rock meets spade and fertile goodness comes only where there has been a carrying of soil with horse and cart, so that there may be a depth for vegetables to root and a hold for the gooseberry and the currant bushes. And there must be watering, for the sun scorches hot on the sides of the hills and green plants wilt away and ever the colour of the fields becomes a brownness, and the sun is said to be scorching the grass again. The fields have a crinkle and crispness and only with rain will the old colour come back. But by the sides of the mountain streams there is the edging of greenness and in the valley the rivers water cattle even when the ponds dry and become cracked, dry patterned mud. Streams which have always the good water meadows and where rushes grow all the year and the alders dip cool root and reach low with shady leaf. Streams where otters live, stone to stone, and perhaps where beavers built dam once, long ago.

Up to the time of the Norman Conquest beavers were found in Welsh rivers. But even at this time they were becoming extinct. Earlier, in the laws of Howel Dda who died in 948, the beaver's pelt was valued at 120 pence while a fox and otter skin were priced only at eightpence. The Welsh called the animal Llostlydan, the Broad-Tailed One. By 1188 the River Teivy in Cardiganshire was the only place in Wales where beavers were to be found. Pennant, the traveller in Wales, mentions haunts where the beaver was once said to live, in the Nant Francon Pass and near Llanrwst on the Conway river.

A fur coat is an ambition of the women of the villages. A thing to swagger to chapel and easily afforded only by the doctor's wife or the wife of some retired city businessman. There is much dressing among the women for fashion competition in the chapels. And always at the time of the preaching meeting or the singing festival there must be worn a new hat or a special coat. The wives who work all week in old darned dresses and thick, woollen, black stockings and ankle-high boots; boots kept supple and soft by fowl-grease painted on hot with a little brush. On working days women who are untidy and rough with hair tied up in any old bun or skewered any way for convenience. Feeding the calves or the chickens and the oldest of clothes worn, fragrant with the smell of the hay loft after the clambering in search of hen eggs. Clothes worn for the milking and with the grassy smell from the cows.

But on Sunday a grand rig-out. The men-folk generally in sober blues and black, but the women have the models bought from market town. A stalk down the aisle, exhibition and the nose-up stares. And she who plays the organ often is a woman who leads the chapel fashion. She who is perched out there in the conspicuous place all the service, for the organ is generally situated centrally in front of the Big Seat and in line with the pulpit.

Gay, glorious hats, veiled and feathered and ripe with cherry. And shoes, those dainty awkward things for walking across a field muddy in winter or staining grass and dusty in the summer. Generally an old pair are worn to walk to the main road and the Sunday-best are carried under arm in a cardboard box. And by the road the change is made and the old walking shoes are stored in the box and hid in the leaning grasses of the hedge bottom, or pushed in the loose hay of a stack.

Daughters of the Welsh farms, black-haired and glamour-stockinged to chapel. For that is the social place and there and in the meetings of the Young Farmers' Clubs will the sweetheart be met. A walking home together after Sunday evening service or after some chapel social. Or after a lecture at the Youth Club which some of the Welsh organisations are running now.

Sunday dress parade, a fine-feather day. But the hands are rough from hard water and the nails have not the dainty half-moons or the crescent points, but are brittled down with outside farm work and the blackleading of a two-ovened kitchen range.

And there is a brown mark on the lengths of the arm above the elbow, there where the sunshine tanned and freckled last harvest time; days of work out in the stubbled fields with cotton dress and old brown shoes. Not much time for perm and lipstick; a smear for the social itches strange and tastes sick with perfume.

Once the dress was the tall hat and the full flowing dress, but the distinctive Welsh woman's dress has disappeared, except for show on the national occasion. The tall hat was said to have been introduced by the Flemings when they emigrated to parts of South Wales in the time of Henry I. Later they came up to Montgomeryshire and took an active part in founding the flannel trade there.

Welsh weddings are teetotal affairs, with the minister as toast-master for water or lukewarm tea. Christenings are done in the Big Seat, at the little table there. The water held in a fancy bowl which the mother has bought specially for the occasion and which is kept afterwards in a safe place on the glass shelf of the china cabinet in the front parlour. To be used again, perhaps, or to be looked at as souvenir of that Sunday afternoon of white shawls and sacred drops of water. From the caretaker's house and with the chill taken off, but believed to have all power under the nervous white hands of the new young minister.

The end of my journey is coming now and the house on the sunny side of the hill by the sea is waiting.

But before I reach the edge of Merionethshire where I now live, yet I must look north to the mountains of Snowdonia. Land of rock and climb and a place, too, which the fairies have not quite neglected. For near Beddgelert on Drws y Coed mountain is a place much loved by the Little People, and it was here that a young farmer married one of them, Penelope.

And it was in the mountains of Caernarvonshire that the tired old giant and his wife dropped their stones. They who were walking through the Pass of Bwlch y Ddeufaen on their way to the Isle of Anglesey. Here in this Pass they met a man who said that he had just walked from the fair island and that his shoes were worn quite through with the labour. The giant and his wife looked in despair at the shoes and the giantess opened out her great apron and the rocks fell out. Rocks which she and her husband were going to use as stepping-stones to place in the sea so that they might cross easily into Anglesey.

The *Gentleman's Magazine* for August 1808 mentions the inn at Beddgelert as having in its visitors' book much verse written by those who had climbed Snowdon. It is recorded that one Dr.

B—k left this entry:

"Dr. B—k stopt the night."

The next entry elaborated on this with the following:

"In Scripture we're told
That Joshua of old
Stopt the day while he thrashed the Philistines;
Here all Wales was in fright—
Dr. B. stopt the night
Whilst he stayed to refresh his intestines."

Many of the old inns of Wales have records of famous travellers who have been guests.

Near Conway there was at the end of the last century the inn where Dean Swift is supposed to have stayed the night always on his way from Dublin. And in gratitude for the comfort and hospitality he had there he wrote verses for either side of the inn's signboard.

A Llangollen hotel has verses by Daniel O'Connell. And Charles Kingsley wrote doggerel in a visitors' book at a Penygwryd inn, but the pages have been stolen.

With the end of the coaching days many of the inns which were on the main highways became little used. And the demand for liquors locally was insufficient to justify a licence. And always the Nonconformists in Wales were active to campaign against a redundant licence, so that many of the inns became private houses. Yards once open to the road were fenced in and the cobblestones in the wonderful fancy shapes and patterns were levered up and a lawn laid. But many of the cobble yards remain, wonderful in diamond pattern and set with white stones carried from the sea or some river bank. A hard-wearing surface and the only worry the weeding out of the grasses which grow quickly in the margins of earth between the shape of the stones. In my old home it was a job to be done sitting cross-legged on a folded meal sack. Using an old jagged, broken table knife and a levering up of the grasses and weeds by the root. For weed-killer was not over-popular and even the harmless variety regarded as a deadly poison, shrivelling and browning as it did all plants good and bad. It was the local plumber who thought of the quick way to remove grass in his own cobbled back yard. He used the flame from his blow-lamp and soon all the village did the same, the plumber having a busy time instructing the difficult art of lighting these roaring, devilish things.

The inns on the distances of the country roads between one village and the next, once important to the horse travellers, these have mostly gone. And the few remaining are gaudy and bravely gay with porcelain-topped petrol pumps and adverts for cigarettes and high tea. The cellar doors flush with the yard surface rear open seldom now. And the vast stabling at the back is used to store old broken furniture and paraffin, or left perhaps just empty. Halter rings rust; and old dung is brown and hard in the spaces between the flooring bricks. On the pegs hang the stiff brush and the short-toothed metal comb which were used by the ostlers and the wagoners to rub and clean the horses. The horse trough in the yard is never filled now from the rattling pump and the inside bottom has a greenness where the last water has evaporated away in the summer sunshine and left its green scum behind.

Cars garage in the old coach-house. Two old tarnished lamps hang from the hooks. Before a car was bought my parents still used a horse and trap. And the lamps at either side were lit at night. Candles inserted inside into long sockets; the tube could be pushed higher as the candles burned away. Wind and rain but the candles always burned well, swaying a bit with the jogging of the horse, and not much use except as a guidance to the width of the trap for those who came to meet us.

To-day only the eccentric ride the countryside in horse and trap. And if the harness breaks suddenly there is only one saddler in ten miles who can repair it. Only one who knows the shape of hooks, the length of straps. Work for the saddlers is becoming less, what with tractors and the coming of cars. Mostly they are middle-aged or old men. And they have no young improvers, no apprentices, and when they die there can be no replacing.

Saddlers' shops with the smell of leather and hanging outside the new-made horse collars, black and lined inside with white cloth, ready for sale. Reins and buckles and straps of all shapes, many sizes. And often now the saddler sells new suitcases and cabin trunks. His art having to move from the repair of girths and the cunning stitching of a hunting saddle to the repair of handbags and the making of zip-fastened "hold-alls". In the market towns the saddler finds a ready sale for these, wonderfully finished and better made than any advertised luggage goods from the London stores. But the village saddlers have to turn to boot and shoe repairing and the fixing on of rubber heels. They who wax thread and can sew on a loose sole waterproof to a sound upper, repair work which the professional city shoe repairer says cannot be done.

Sometimes a saddle comes in for repair or a well-made bridle to be altered. Some farmer's daughter is determined to ride at the local agricultural show and wants to use the saddle found in the loft. The saddler can do that. Takes a joy in it, for not often does this work come his way. The hunting is almost finished and there are no racing stables to give constant work.

A joy in shaping leather, in the even spacing of stitch holes. Fingers making a pattern of soft leather, a shape to last sweat of horse and beat of rain for a score of years. Thread which will not rot with snow or sunshine; for this is named work and all know that the grey head could not show proud in the village if the saddle breaks or the cart-horse warps a collar with any strain.

And the Welsh name over the shop could not be painted so proudly new each year if there had been any failure, any time when the skilful hands had not done their work good and true.

Snowdonia of mountains and lakes and climbs and views to the north of England, and to the south of Wales where the lilting-tongued ones live. This steep country with gully and great cavern cleft and mist and a loving, lingering snow. This tourist play-ground for those who love mountains, the sheer rise of rock places.

Snowdon, the main peak, is 3,571 feet high and is surrounded by four slightly lesser peaks; Crib y Pistell, Crib Goch, Llyn Llydaw and the ridge of Lliwedd.

After the conquest of Wales Edward I made a Royal Forest of the Snowdonia district. And near Llanberis is Dolbadarn Castle, only a tower of a place, but dungeoned and where Owain Goch was kept a prisoner by his brother for twenty-three years in the thirteenth century. At Beddgelert a noble hound is supposed to lie, but this a piece of propaganda invented in Victorian days.

Romantic Snowdon, highest peak of Wales or England. Noble mountain, advert for the north-west of Wales. A beckoning finger to mountaineers and sightseers. To those who want to see the sun-rise from high places, watch the shine of mountain lakes at night. Come now, they have catered for you wisely. Tourist and traveller and fisherman, come, for the beds are comfortable. And if you fall in gully steep or get lost in the haunting mists they have plans to help and find you. Stretchers ready and those who know the mountains, know it when the mists swirl and make the phantom shapes. When the wind beats the rain with an echoing patter on the rocks, and when the foot slips and there is no support for the nailed boot. Shapes and new shadows coming to the mountain, a toughness when the holiday mood is tucked away and spite comes with the rain and a slipping foothold. A place grand to the palm when the sun hits hot in June, and the waves of heat are cooled by the mountain wind; wind which makes tempting music round rock corner and across the wide steep places.

All is waiting for the holiday climber. Come up Snowdon the

steep path or up the easier mountain railway, with its ratchet cogs and hotel at the top. Or climb steep reaches of rock, with rope and strain of body.

Climb Snowdon, those who are not content to watch sunrise in level, smooth places. Those who want to see the sun making black shapes of old mountains. Those who want the view distant of far-off places, strange countries and distance made small and the eye a telescope. Those who are not satisfied with the red sea sunset and that last flash of green as the sun sinks. Or those who see no beauty in city sunset, with the dirt sky splitting up the last light into countless red rays. Those who hurry home in bus and tube and train, with never a look to the West London sky or the sunset over Mersey Bar. But come anxious to the heights to see the first and last of the sun. But missing from the bleak height all the countryman's thrill of first dawn, the swelling bird song of the valleys and the shires. Only the unreal majesty of craggy sunrise from Snowdon and all pulse of life halted for the great act. With tea and coffee and breakfast waiting.

All well organised for the holiday. Snowdonia wants you. The posters are brilliant and the little Switzerland will collect the litter and lay clean sheets. Any day now will someone think of the Birmingham twinkle of a cow bell, and there will be yodelling at the Eisteddfod, and a real live Welsh Swiss Miss.

Away from Snowdonia and back to the edge of the sea, the coast road again. The sea and the slope of the fields away from the turn of the tide. Wales with its coast; the sea and Davy Jones and his Locker, dread of all sailors. A connection, surely?

Sailors believe that Davy Jones is the chief spirit of all the evil ones of the deep places. He who shows himself only when death is near. His name is said to be a corruption of Jonah, "duffy Jonah", duffy, a special ghost of the West Indians.

Yet parts of Wales claim Davy Jones. The legend is that as Noah was floating his Ark a human was seen on a rock, calling and shouting and who eventually came swimming to the side of the Ark. He was told they were full up, no room. The man then threw up to Noah himself a small package which he said was the pedigree of David Jones to the time of Adam. The Ark lurched on and the keel sank poor David Jones and he was not seen again.

I sit on the edge of a little cliff, where the little hazel stems and the leaning gorse grow in the gullies of the rock. Sit there with a view across the sea, the level sand from cliff bottom to the first distant breakers. Sit and wait for the turn of the tide. Dangle legs to the sea winds, cool and cold as if from some sea cellar bottom.

A look below to the old rope, coiled and twisted and thrown up
by the last tide, all goodness rotted away. And all the half-buried
treasure of the sand. A cardboard box with only its straight rims
showing and having all the shape and magic of Spain.

The broken walking stick ridged round with sand and a great
black tail of seaweed caught round the handle. The sea and the
sand and the distance making a half-cloak, half-dagger of it. And
beyond, far beyond on the loose, wet sand, the broken shape of
the ship's boat, half in sand, half in air. The opened sides through
which the tide hums and moans twice every day. The paint long
washed away and now the cunningly-shaped wood has a whiteness, save where the barnacles cling, rough and black and un-
patterned on the whiteness. Ribs open, through which the wind
blows now, soon where the sea will come again, now that the tide
has turned and aches to meet my cliff again. Old broken boat, left

there all the years. Once in from the sea, they say, and left behind on a dull angry morning when the wind had blown all night and the rain had made frightened noises on the window panes, and all the roofs had had the trickle of water. Butt and tank overflowing and the wind easing away only with the morning, but still to sea the white, dancing horses, a prance to the greenness.

This boat left when the tide had gone sullenly out. A new boat, they said, good and sound. And through their glasses they had looked from the top of the cliffs to see if there was man in it. But she was empty, stuck there on the dangerous sand. No one could go out to her, for the sand shook and the feet would sink fast there. All top golden colour a varnish only; underneath all black and every little hole oozing water.

The boat out there all the years. Each month a little deeper, some of the woodwork taken away. Sent drifting out to sea; brave brass screwed, but torn away by some tide of the night, some urging sea of the day.

And there are the other things, too, on the flat sand between my cliff and the sea. Black trunks of washed-up trees, stark as coal on the sand. And a great pipe set firm among piles on the sand; sewage, and around the trickling mouth of it the gulls wait, perching and preening.

A small boy flying a kite, catching the breeze from the sea. He stands a hundred yards out. As he moves he watches to see that he does not walk to the shifting sands where the skeleton boat is buried. Sometimes he turns to look at the cliff and then again to the sea as it moves slowly in to the land. The boy who lives by the sea and does not trust its dangerous ways.

Sheep, nimble-footed, graze the lawn tops of the cliffs to the sides of me. Sure-footed to reach verdant rich-shaded grass. And having deep little sanded holes to sleep in, and for shelter when the west wind blows hard from the sea.

Sheep were once milked in Wales, a highly-skilled job. The milk is said to be one of the most nutritious and too strong for general use, having to be diluted with cows' milk. Puddings were made from it, and also white butter and excellent cheese. The sheeps' milk was said to produce twice the weight of cheese as the equivalent quantity of cows' milk. The sheep milking was done from the middle of May until the end of August and the lowland sheep gave two to three pints in twenty-four hours. The hardier mountain sheep gave only about half a pint in that period.

Cheese was once made extensively on Welsh farms. In Burton's *History of the Principality of Wales*, published in 1695, we read:

"Then they have cheese very tender and palatable the pedigree whereof was by one thus merrily derived 'Adam's nawn Cusson was by her Birth ap Curds, ap Milk, ap Cow, ap Grass, ap Earth'. They have likewise Metheglin, first invented by Matthew Glin, their own countryman, it is compounded of milk and honey, and very wholesome. Pollio Romulus, being an hundred years of age, told Julius Cæsar 'That he had preserved the vigour of his mind and body by taking Metheglin inwardly and using Oyl outwardly'. It is like Mead but much stronger. Queen Elizabeth, who by the Tudors was of Welsh Descent, much loved this her native liquor."

The art of cheese-making is not practised now. But in the yards of many of the larger farms still stand the disused cheese presses. A spouted stone trough set in an iron framework with a round stone fixing into it at the end of a screw. The whey was pressed out of the cheese by the turning of a wooden handle at the top of the press, this forcing the one stone down into the trough, the whey spouting and used for animal feeding. Rusted now the cheese press, and green fancy moss old and untouched on the grey stone. The screw creaks if turned and all the cheese is bought from the grocery van calling punctual twice a week. Or brought home from market, a whole cheese in its muslin.

Hanging on one side of the hearth, too, are the cheese samplers. Now bright polished brass and ornamental. A long rod, round-ended and with a small handle. This tool used to drive deep into the heart of the cheese to test the quality.

And now that the corn is threshed quickly, or stored in the gal-vanised-roofed Dutch barns, the great stones which once held the ricks high off the ground as a protection against rats and damp, these have become ornaments or used for other ways. The mush-room-shaped stones in two pieces, a conical stalk, and fitting on top a round, flat headstone. The latter make excellent grindstones and many of the farmers have pierced the centre of one of these and set a handle through and fixed the stone to turn in a stand. A grindstone for sharpening axes and chisels and the curved blades used for the hedge cutting. Sometimes the scythe blades are shar-pened on the grindstone, the first thickness of the blunt blade taken away ready for the final whetting by hand. The snead held between the legs in the hand sharpening, the blade pointing away from the shoulder. And alternate strokes made with a hand whet-stone on either side of the blade, to the point on one side and back on the other side. A familiar sound in the Welsh countryside, this "whep-whep" of a scythe being sharpened, the sound across the fields or down from a hillside. A smooth regularity and this scythe sharpening not easily learned. Scythes as still used for fern cutting, for man and swinging blade can reach places when the horse mowing machines cannot turn. And scythes are used for thistle cutting and to cut hay in the corners and sides of the fields at harvest time. And used, too, to make an entrance way into the first few yards of corn near the gate. A place so that the tractor and self-binder can draw in without trampling corn. And the scythes are used in orchards, in the awkward distances between the trees. And used to cut the stray nettles and weeds clumping green and untidy around the farm buildings.

Butter is made on the mountain farms. And by the flavour and the colour the farmer's wife knows the pasture which the cows have grazed. Sweet buttercups or harsh dandelion. Green rich grass growing fast in fields after the hay cutting or the tough wiry pasture where there has been no harvesting, no ploughing and no re-seeding.

Coming the way along the coast, the road from the north through Harlech and down to Barmouth. The road home, the last way. The stone-walled road with the green of stunted fir trees and the grey, small-windowed farmhouses. Cows graze in the little fields, all view of the bay hidden by the height of the stone walls. Fields warm and with all wind kept away and only the sunshine allowed in. Fields with all the warmth of a walled, country-house garden. But already the caravans are coming. One or two in the snug fields. Fresh and smart with paint, setting up by some little stream where it trickles the round boulders and smooth-rubbed stones down to the sea. Fresh water for the cooking and the washing, and ever the sea a few yards away for the first shivering paddle, the first awkward swim of the year.

The caravans are coming to the lonely coast. Perhaps last year it was the holiday in Aberdovey or Barmouth or Portmadoc. They have loved the loneliness and comes an urge often for a week-end by this sea. So the car brings the trailer caravan and is set up, a fat rent for the farmer from his field. Or perhaps the hideous height of an old city double-decker bus is brought in and set up, towering above the sand. The strips of adverts painted out, paint chosen surely for the brightness, the glare of its colour.

They are lonely enough yet, the distances between the estuaries. But the caravans are coming to the sides of the sea. Old shacks will come in hundreds soon, with tented lavatories and colours which even the salt wind of the sea cannot soothe away. But those who fight sham and ugliness are watching. And the time must come when the camps and shacks will have to fester in one place only, and leave the miles lonely and undecorated.

I go the road home. The sea by my side, and beyond that, to the west, old Ireland. The Irish who are a dearer, sweeter people to the Welsh than any of the English who live beyond the sunrise. Perhaps it is the sea, the border barrier. No easy reaching across, but once in a while come the stray little ships from the Irish ports. Masted and weather-worn and coming into the harbours of West Wales doing nobody's business. On the decks the lashed drums of engine oil and through the cabin skylights the peep of dishes and the drift of pipe smoke.

On into Barmouth again. Here where all the sun is cupped between sea and the high grey cliff above the uneven town. The surf roars and the sands are gay with summer. Colour and spades and arm-in-arm. Splash and high kick in Cardigan Bay. Swimmers coming in with the tide and on the long green, benches the old ones sit, curve of wood to aching back. Pleasure boats, old ships' lifeboats, chug out to sea, a flag dangling brave and laundered new at the back. And a man at the long brown tiller, a man in a blue jersey and with a jaunty white-roofed cap angled to his cigaretted ear. Sometimes his foot reaches out and the noise of the motor chugs less, and then reaches a new regularity, the water blows white from the bow. And the boat is full of holiday-makers, those for the quiet holiday in Wales. Coming to the places where sea and sand are the main attractions and lights aim no short cut to wattage fairyland.

A dog plays a stick in the sea, angry and barking as the wood

twists and sways away. Two young, white-flapping girls are looking for ices. No ices on the beach? Hot and loose-sandaled they
walk into the town, peeved and silent. Forgetting that to-night
with the first wink of sleep they can hear the beat of bird wing; or
rise in the night and see the moon reflected and stretched away,
edging the top of a hundred little waves. Or watch the stars twinkle
over Ireland itself, with not a yellow-lit light between the two
Celtic lands; or watch a curtain rustle in the wind, the first grip
of breeze to land, wind which has blown south-west from far
beyond the curve of Ireland, wind from the far Atlantic places and
now come with a shake into Wales.

But ices? No ices near the beach? And not a pub open on a
Sunday. Wales, indeed, with its grim chapels and the black-
clothed ones.

But the sea and the mountains, the places where water and
heather meet sky? Wales, too, and pub and chapel lose shape and
sign, become grey, and known only as stone.

I go home to where Merionethshire joins the sea. The house by
the salt water with the view of the far, high mountains. And beyond the mountains is the Border country, the first edge of the
Wales where I was born.

That country with the neat patchwork fields and always the
view of distant Shropshire from every rise in the ground. Slow
rivers and well-ordered farms, gentle first hills of Wales.

Here it is sand and sea and the heap of mountains. And the
English only come in the summer.

Now through my window the sea shimmers summer evening
still. And the oyster-catchers stand on the sandbanks out in the
estuary, grouped black and white and ready to fly away when the
seawater laps their feet.

Behind my house there is a small wooded hill. The one side bare
to the sea with only stunted saplings bending always away from
the wind; the wet west wind which blows wild here, sending the
rain slinging to the face. Rattling the slates which the landlord
tells me have been like that all the years, always loose, always
rattling. The wind which rattles the slates, shakes the old sash
windows, makes bare the one side of my hill. They call it the
Fegla, the Sea Barrier. And though now the sea reaches the
smooth bottom rocks only with the January and October tides,
yet once every tide, every day, reached my hill. Sucking
and smoothing and rolling little stones twice in the twenty-four
hours.

But the other side of the hill is wooded. Small tight-topped oaks with the blaze of red foxgloves under them in the summer. Green nettles wave as a grass snake moves.

Climbing my hill through the trees I see the yellow of the sands, the bright waving blue of the sea. Colours bright between the trees. And at the top of the hill there is the sudden drop, the sudden view. West across the sea I can see Bardsey, a blue wart on the end of the blue Lleyn Peninsula.

East are the mountains, gaunt and certain shaped, brown-sided, grey-rocked, and a pattern one behind the other into the distance.

Here on top of my hill someone has fixed a great iron bar into the top rock. A hole drilled and the base of the bar has been set deep. And with the years the sea air and the salt flying before the wind has worn rusted notches in the iron; carved crevices and made a roughness.

The bar clangs in a high wind and at a touch comes a hum and a quiver.

I lean on the bar, look out to Bardsey. Turn and look over the estuary to the mountains losing colour, losing shape with the last daylight.

The tide has turned and the sandbanks, made dry by the wind, grow smaller and become evenly covered.

On the coast road the first lights come, and black in the sky the first gulls fly inland for the night.

The little wind that comes with the end of the day moans the small stunted trees and blows on to the height of Cader Idris, black behind me to the blue night sky. The first stars come; the last edge of the sea is lost in dimness and only a light from one of the shore houses streaks long waving yellow across the incoming tide. With the night comes a coldness. I go down the hill. Down to where the sea licks the rocks and where I live now, the red house by the sea at the end of my journey.

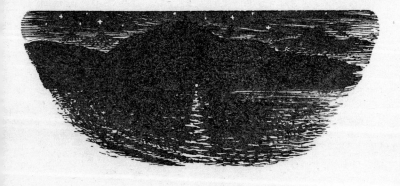

BIBLIOGRAPHY

A Tour Through the Whole Island of Great Britain, 1724–1726, Daniel Defoe
A Tour in Wales, 1778–1781, Thomas Pennant
Tours in Wales, 1784 and 1787, *The Torrington Diaries*, John Byng, 1934 edition
A Pedestrian Tour Through North Wales, 1795, J. Hucks
A Tour Round North Wales, 1798, William Bingley
Wild Wales, 1854, George Borrow
Welsh Folk Lore, 1896, Elias Owen
Highways and Byways in North Wales, 1898, A. G. Bradley
The Welsh People, 1900, John Rhys and Brynmor Jones
A Wayfarer in Wales, 1930, W. Watkin Davies
Tramping Through Wales, 1931, John C. Moore
In Search of Wales, 1932, H. V. Morton
Wales, 1932, W. T. Palmer
On Foot in Wales, 1934, Patrick Monkhouse
Out With the Cambrians, 1934, Evelyn Lawes
The Blue Guide to Wales, 1936
The Land of Wales, 1937, Eiluned and Peter Lewis
Welsh Border Country, 1938, Thoresby Jones
Gossiping Guide to Wales, 1938, Askew Roberts and Forward Woodhall
Walking Through Merionethshire, 1939, Hope Hewett
Over Welsh Hills, 1941, F. S. Smythe
The Welsh Three Thousands, 1947, Thomas Firbank
The Mountains of Snowdonia in History, the Sciences, Literature, and Sport, 1948, edited by H. R. C. Carr and G. A. Lister
A Prospect of Wales, 1949, Gwyn Jones and Kenneth Rowntree

INDEX

Long. 4°W.

Amlwch

Holyhead

ANGLESEY

Red Wharf
Bay

Puffin I

Llanfairfechan

MENAI BRIDGE

Aber

Bangor

Caernarvon

N

W   E

S

SNOWDON

Lat. 53°N

Tremadoc

Ffestiniog

Nevin

Criccieth

CAERNAR

Pwllheli

Harlech

Aberdaron

CAER

M   E

Llanelll

Bardsey
Island

CARDIGAN

Llanaber

Barmouth

Fairbourne

CADER

Llwyngwril

BAY

Towyn

Aberdovey

Statute   Miles

5   10   15   20

Aberystwyth